C I T Y P A C K
Prague

By Michael Ivory

Fodor's

Fodor's Travel Publications
New York • Toronto • London • Sydney • Auckland

HTTP://WWW.FODORS.COM/

Contents

About this book

ORGANIZATION

Citypack Prague's six sections cover the six most important aspects of your visit to Prague:

- Prague life—the city and its people
- Itineraries, walks, and excursions—how to organize your time
- The top 25 sights, numbered 1–25 from west to east across the city
- Features about different aspects of the city that make it special
- Detailed listings of restaurants, hotels, shops, and nightlife
- Practical information

In addition, text boxes provide fascinating extra facts and snippets, highlights of places to visit, and invaluable practical advice.

CROSS-REFERENCES

To help you make the most of your visit, cross-references, indicated by ► , show you where to find additional information about a place or subject.

MAPS

- The fold-out map in the wallet at the back of the book is a comprehensive street plan of Prague. All the map references given in the book refer to this map. For example, the National Theater on Národní 2, Nové město, has the following information: ✠ D/E5—indicating the grid squares of the map in which the National Theater will be found.
- The city-center maps found on the inside front and back covers of the book itself are for quick reference. They show the Top 25 Sights, described on pages 24–48, which are clearly plotted by number (**1** – **25**, not page number) from west to east.

PRICES

Where appropriate, an indication of the cost of an establishment is given by **$** signs: **$$$** denotes higher prices, **$$** denotes average prices, while **$** denotes lower charges.

PRAGUE
life

INTRODUCING PRAGUE

St. Nicholas's Church, seen from Hradčany

"Golden Prague," "Prague the hundred-towered," "the most beautiful city in Europe": such clichés are certainly true, though they tell only part of the story. Ocher in color, many of the city's buildings can gleam like gold, especially in the glow of the late afternoon sun; the skyline is punctuated by the uncountable towers, turrets, and steeples; and Prague's beauty is incontestable.

The site is superb, with rock bluffs above a broad and curving river, and steep slopes rising through orchards and woodland. Human activities have enhanced what Nature provided so generously, crowning the heights with great churches and palaces, emphasizing the slopes with terraced gardens, precipitous streets, and flights of stairs, and marking the course of the river with a sequence of foaming weirs and bold bridges.

Over a thousand years of history is expressed in stone: the foundations of the first Christian churches can still be seen, while below the sidewalks of the Old Town are vaulted cellars that once formed the ground floor of medieval merchants' houses. In the 17th and 18th centuries the Baroque style transformed the city's appearance. In the 19th century came great landmarks such as the National Museum and National Theater—testimony to the Czech nation's self-confidence—followed by the extravagances of art nouveau. Even the radical architects of the first half of the 20th century managed to insert their innovative buildings into the urban scene with a minimum of disturbance.

Urban decay

Visitors are sometimes shocked at the shabby state of some of Prague's buildings. Under Communism, showpieces were restored at great public expense, but less favored buildings moldered away, encased in straitjackets of scaffolding to stop them falling into the street. Privatization and restitution (the return of property to its former owners) has gone far to remedy the situation.

In spite of (or perhaps as a result of) military defeats, occupation, and denial of citizens' rights, the four distinct quarters that form Prague's historic core are in a near-perfect state of preservation. They are the Castle district (Hradčany), the Lesser Town (Malá Strana) at its foot, the Old Town (Staré město) across the river, and the New Town (Nové město) laid out in the 14th century.

Beyond is a ring of rundown suburbs, largely 19th-century, then an outer circle of high-rise housing projects and satellite towns built during the last 40 years. These suburbs are where most Praguers live. For many, life after Communism remains grey the struggle to make ends meet greater than ever. Others have embraced the new freedom with alacrity; there's an obvious enjoyment in the previously forbidden pleasures of making and spending money. The continuing stream of visitors from abroad adds an extra element of vibrancy and has vastly improved the places to eat and to stay. Entrepreneurs are everywhere, opening shops, cafés, and bars. There's excitement in the air, particularly among the young, as Prague claims its rightful place in a Europe from which it has been long excluded.

Get lost

Prague is a labyrinth, a warren of winding roads and alleyways, courtyards and passageways leading deep into buildings. Don't worry about getting lost—treat disorientation as a pleasure and enjoy the unexpected treats along the way. The historic center is small, and sooner or later you will recognize a landmark or emerge by the riverside.

Míšeňská Street, Malá Strana

PRAGUE IN FIGURES

GEOGRAPHY

- Prague, located in Central Europe and situated on the River Vltava, is the capital of the Czech Republic (and until 1993 was the capital of Czechoslovakia)
- Prague lies 50° 5' north and 14° 25' east
- Area: 191 square miles
- Lowest point (River Vltava): 577 feet above sea-level
- Highest point (Kopanina): 1,299 feet above sea-level
- Distance from Berlin: 217 miles
- Distance from Vienna: 181 miles
- Distance from Paris: 643 miles
- Distance from London: 853 miles

PEOPLE

- Population: 1,225,000; 95.5 percent are of Czech nationality
- Living conditions: about half the population lives in *paneláks*, the high-rise apartments built under Communism. The largest housing project is "Southwest Town," with a planned population that should reach a total of 140,000 inhabitants
- Nearly half of Prague's population leaves the city on summer weekends, many to spend time in their *chata*, or country cottage
- 43,000 students attend universities in the city

ENVIRONMENT

- Conservation: the city's historic core, designated by UNESCO as being of world importance, covers an area of 2,224 acres and includes some 10,000 protected artifacts and works of art
- The city has nearly 25,000 acres of green spaces (parks, cemeteries, etc.)
- Nearly 750,000 vehicles fill the 1,738 miles of city streets. Prague's Metro, 27 miles long and with 46 stations, carries more than a third of all the city's public transportation passengers. There are more than 80 miles of tram lines within the city
- Prague is a heavily polluted city. Its industries, heating plants, and motor vehicles emit more than 30,000 tons of sulfur dioxide per annum

PRAGUE PEOPLE

VÁCLAV HAVEL

Playwright and one-time prominent dissident President Havel, by attempting to combine political activity with ethical principles, has not always endeared himself to market-obsessed politicians keen to rush the new republic into the embrace of modern capitalism. Gruff of voice and short of stature, Havel has survived ill-treatment by secret police and a chain-smoking past, but his shaky state of health is a cause for concern for many citizens, who see him as an irreplaceable asset to this fledgling democracy.

IVAN PLICKA

Engineer Plicka has spent most of his working life in the section of the City Architect's Department responsible for the planning of Greater Prague. Now near retirement, he is proud of the city's beauty and of his office's role in preserving it. He hopes his department's forthcoming masterplan to take Prague into the next millennium will protect the downtown area from the commercial pressures that have destroyed the traditional character of many western cities.

Engineer Ivan Plicka

LENKA CHOBOTOVÁ

Lively Lenka, one of a generation of young people who experienced Communism only as a small child, graduated from a high school specializing in information sciences. A six-month stay in Britain gave her fluency in English, and she hopes to study English literature at one of Prague's universities, though for the time being she is happy to earn a modest living as a librarian. Cheerful and outgoing, Lenka has a zest for life that expresses itself in getting together with like-minded friends to sing and make music in one of the city's innumerable pubs.

Jo Williams

Art historian Jo hails from New York City and is one of a number of young Americans attracted to post-Communist Prague. An enthusiast for Czech culture, she has not only mastered the language but works in a Czech environment at a local salary, helping to raise the profile of an arts foundation. Her first job involved promoting abroad the hidden treasures of the National Gallery's modern art collection in the Veletržní palác.

A Chronology

7th or 8th century AD	Prague's legendary foundation by Princess Libuše and her plowman husband, Přemysl
Late 9th century	A Slav stronghold is established on Hradčany Hill, where Prince Bořivoj builds the first timber church
10th century	Trading settlements are established in Lesser Town (Malá Strana) and Old Town (Staré město)
1231	King Wenceslas I fortifies the Old Town with 13 towers, 39-foot-high walls, and a moat (today's Na příkopě, or Moat Street)
1253–1278	Reign of King Otakar II, who extends and fortifies Malá Strana, inviting German merchants and traders to settle there
1346–1378	Under King/Emperor Charles IV, St. Vitus's Cathedral is begun, the New Town (Nové město) is laid out, and Charles Bridge is built
1415	Religious reformer Jan Hus is burned at the stake for heresy
1576–1611	Reign of eccentric Emperor Rudolph II
1620	Battle of the White Mountain just outside Prague, in which the Protestant army is routed. In the following years, Protestant leaders are executed in Old Town Square. Czechs who refuse to reconvert to Catholicism emigrate en masse. A largely foreign nobility is installed, loyal to the Habsburgs, and Prague is beautified with Baroque churches and palaces. The court makes Vienna its principal seat, and Prague becomes a sleepy provincial town
1848	A revolt led by students is put down by Austrian General Windischgrätz, but Czech nationalism continues to grow
1914–1918	Czechs are dragged into World War I on the Austrian side. Many soldiers desert or join the Czech Legion fighting for the Allies in Russia, Italy, and France

1918 Establishment of the democratic First Republic of Czechoslovakia under liberal President Tomáš Masaryk

1938 Britain and France agree to cede the Sudetenland to Hitler's Germany, depriving Czechoslovakia of most of its industry and all its defenses

1939 Hitler dismembers what is left of Czechoslovakia. The Czech provinces become the "Protectorate of Bohemia-Moravia," and Prague is declared the "Fourth City of the Third Reich"

1942 The assassination of Reichsprotektor Heydrich by Czechoslovak parachutists flown in from Britain leads to brutal repression by the Nazis

1945 The people of Prague liberate their city and welcome in the Red Army. More than 2.5 million Germans are expelled from the Sudetenland

1948 Communists, the most powerful party in the democratically elected government, stage a coup d'état. Stalinist repression follows

1968 The Prague Spring, an attempt to change Communism into "Socialism with a human face," is crushed by Soviet tanks

1977 Dissident intellectuals sign Charter 77, a call for the government to apply the Helsinki Agreements of 1975. Many, including Václav Havel, are harrassed and imprisoned on trumped-up charges

1989 The Velvet Revolution. The Communist government resigns and is replaced by the dissident-led Civic Forum. Václav Havel is elected president

1993 Czechoslovakia splits into the independent states of Slovakia and the Czech Republic (with Prague as the latter's capital)

1997 The Czech economy stalls and the government falls amid corruption accusations

11

PEOPLE & EVENTS FROM HISTORY

Fall from power

Yet another Prague defenestration (not officially referred to as such) was the fall of much-loved foreign minister Jan Masaryk from his office window in the Černín Palace when the Communists seized power in 1948. His opposition to Communism led many to think that he was pushed, but it is more likely that he jumped, in despair at the prospect facing his country and at his powerlessness to prevent it.

Alexander Dubček

DEFENESTRATIONS

Prague's history is marked by several defenestrations—in which political opponents were violently ejected from upper-floor windows. The first, in 1419, seems to have happened spontaneously. A crowd of Hussites demonstrating in Charles Square was pelted with stones from the New Town Hall by their Catholic adversaries, who—to make matters worse—were German. The infuriated mob stormed the building and threw the culprits from the upstairs windows onto the cobbles of the square, where they were brutally killed. A window of the Old Town Hall provided the means for expressing discontent in 1483, when the mayor of Prague was the victim of the second defenestration.

The third defenestration, in 1618, marked the start of the Thirty Years War. A group of Protestant noblemen forcibly entered Prague Castle and hurled a pair of Catholic councellors and their secretary into the dung-heaps that had accumulated in the moat. The victims' survival—the manure broke their fall—was widely attributed to divine intervention.

FALSE SPRING

By the mid-1960s, the oppressiveness of the Communist system in Czechoslovakia was becoming all too apparent. In what came to be known as the "Prague Spring" of 1968, the party under Alexander Dubček promised to create "Socialism with a human face." Terrified at this prospect, the Soviet Union sent in tanks in August and took the government off to Moscow in chains. A humiliated Dubček was first told to reverse his reforms, and then dismissed. Two decades of social and political winter followed, ended by the Velvet Revolution in 1989.

PRAGUE
how to organize your time

ITINERARIES

These itineraries, all beginning from the "Golden Cross"—the pedestrianized area where Wenceslas Square (Václavské náměstí) meets Národní třída and Na příkopě—are based on Prague's four historic districts.

ITINERARY ONE	OLD TOWN & JOSEFOV
Morning	Walk east along Na příkopě (Moat Street) Municipal House (► 46) Walk along Celetná Street to the Old Town Square (Staroměstské náměstí; ► 42) Coffee at one of the cafés in Old Town Square Climb the tower of the Old Town Hall Astronomical Clock (► 59) Take in Týn Church and Týn Court (► 55) Walk along Pařížská (Paris Boulevard) to the Old/New Synagogue (► 39)
Lunch	Restaurant on Pařížská
Afternoon	Old Jewish Cemetery (► 40) Decorative Arts Museum (► 37)
ITINERARY TWO	HRADČANY, THE CASTLE HILL
Morning	Go west along 28 října and Národní streets Catch Tram No. 22 at the Národní třída stop (Bila Hora direction) to the Pohořelec stop Strahov Monastery (► 24) Coffee in Pohořelec Square Continue to the Loretto Shrine (► 26) Follow Černínska Street to Nový Svět (► 25) Prague Castle (► 29)
Lunch	One of the castle restaurants
Afternoon	St. Vitus's Cathedral (► 30) St. George's Basilica and Convent (► 31) Head through Castle Gardens (► 58) and go via Nerudova (► 32) to Malá Strana Square Return to the Golden Cross by Tram No. 22 or on foot across the Charles Bridge
ITINERARY THREE	OVER THE BRIDGE TO MALÁ STRANA
Morning	Enter the Old Town via Na můstku and Havelská ulička, turn left into the market held

on Havelská and V kotcích streets, and
continue west via Uhelný trh and Skořepka
Street into Bethlehem Square
Bethlehem Chapel (► 55)
Náprstek Museum (► 53)
Coffee in café or restaurant on Bethlehem
Square
Follow Husova Street and turn left onto the
Royal Way on Karlova Street
Cross Charles Bridge
Turn right into Josefská Street and again into
Letenská Street
Wallenstein Palace (► 34)

Lunch   Café or restaurant in Malá Strana Square

Afternoon   Sr. Nicholas's Church (► 33)
Schönborn and Lobkovic Palaces (► 54)
Church of Our Lady Victorious (► 55)
Walk via Mostecká and Lázěnská to Maltese
Square and Grand Priors' Square with the John
Lennon Wall
Cross the Čertovka brook to Na kampě on
Kampa Island
Return via Legions' Bridge (Most legií) and
the National Theater (► 36)

ITINERARY FOUR   NEW TOWN & VYŠEHRAD

Morning   Walk west into Jungmann Square
(Jungmannovo náměstí)
Stroll in the Franciscans' Garden
(Františkánská zahrada) behind the Church of
Our Lady of the Snows
Wenceslas Square (► 43); stop for coffee
National Museum (► 44)

Lunch   Restaurant or café in Wenceslas Square

Afternoon   Metro to Vyšehrad
Palace of Culture
Go west along Na Bučance and V pevnosti
Vyšehrad (► 38)
Tram No. 3, then return to Wenceslas Square
via Vodičkova Street and Novák building
(U Novaku; ► 56)

WALKS

THE SIGHTS

- Old Town Hall (➤ 42)
- Clam-Gallas Palace
- Old Town Bridge Tower (➤ 35)
- Charles Bridge (➤ 35)
- St. Nicholas's Church, Malá Strana (➤ 33)
- Neruda Street (➤ 32)

INFORMATION

Distance 1.2 miles
Time 1 hour
Start point Old Town Square (Staroměstské náměstí)
🚇 E4
Ⓜ Staroměstská
End point Hradčany Square (Hradčany náměstí)
🚇 C4
🚌 Tram 22

Surface restoration

With their often ambivalent attitude to tradition, the Communists decided to promote the Royal Way (see Walk) as a tourist route, restoring the buildings along it. But the treatment was sometimes more of a face-lift than a complete rejuvenation.

IN THE FOOTSTEPS OF KINGS—THE OLD TOWN TO THE CASTLE

This walk follows the Royal Way, the ancient coronation route taken by Czech kings from their downtown residence to the cathedral high up in Hradčany. It starts in Old Town Square and is deservedly popular, so you are likely to have plenty of company.

Go west into Little Square (Malé náměstí), with its delightful fountain, and turn into twisting Karlova Street, with its tempting gift shops. The street's final curve brings you into Knights of the Cross Square (Křížovnicke náměstí). Look out for the traffic as you rush to enjoy the incomparable view of the castle across the river.

Pass through the Old Town Bridge Tower onto Charles Bridge; admire the stunning procession of saintly statues that adorns its parapets. As it approaches Malá Strana, the bridge becomes a flyover, and then, after the Malá Strana Bridge Tower, it leads you to Mostecká (Bridge) Street. Cross Malá Strana Square (Malostranské náměstí), dominated by the great bulk of St. Nicholas's Church, with care. Grit your teeth in preparation for the long climb up Nerudova (Neruda Street), and don't forget to turn sharp right onto the final leg of the castle approach, named Ke hradu. Regain your breath while leaning on the wall of Hradčany Square and soak up the panorama of the city far below, a just reward for the climb.

Café in Old Town Square

Ceiling in the Schwarzenberg Palace

BACK TO THE OLD TOWN VIA SOME OF PRAGUE'S GARDENS

From Hradčany Square walk up Loretanská Street, turning 180 degrees left as you enter Pohořelec Square. A short way down Úvoz, make a sharp right and stop to enjoy the view from the vineyard lying just below Strahov Monastery. Go through the monastery courtyard, turning right into Pohořelec, then left into Loretto Square (Loretánské náměstí). Narrow Černinska Street leads downhill into Nový Svět.

Return to Hradčany Square via Nový Svět and Kanovnická. Go through the Matthias Gate of the castle, then out of the north gate from the castle's Second Courtyard. Turn into the Royal Gardens; leave them near the Belvedere summer palace and enter the Chotek Gardens (Chotkovy sady). Cross the footbridge into Letná Plain (Letenské sady), and view the city first from the Hanava Pavilion (Hanavský pavilon) and then from the plinth where Stalin's statue stood. Descend the steps and ramps to the Cech Bridge (Čechův most) and return to Old Town Square via Josefov—the former Jewish ghetto.

Rustic retreat

The tiny vineyard below Strahov Monastery is a leftover from the days when vines clad most of the slopes hereabouts. Young apple, pear, cherry, and almond trees have been planted.

EVENING STROLLS

INFORMATION

The Old Town
Distance 1 mile
Time 1 hour
Start point: National Museum
(Národní muzeum)
🚩 F5
🚇 Muzeum
End point Smetana statue
🚩 D4
🚇 Staroměstská

The New Town
Distance 2 miles
Time 1½ hours
Start and end point
Smetana statue
🚩 D4
🚇 Staroměstská

THE OLD TOWN

Survey the busy downtown scene from the terrace in front of the National Museum at the top of Wenceslas Square (Václavské náměstí) before leaving through the underpass (don't try to cross the road) and walk down either side of the square. Keep going in the same direction at the foot of the square, along Na můstku and Melantrichova into Old Town Square (Staroměstské náměstí). Follow the Royal Way (▶ 16), turning left into Husova Street, then right into Bethlehem Square (Betlémské náměstí), a quieter focus of nightlife. Head down Náprstkova Street and join the Vltava embankment, crossing the road carefully. The best point to absorb the view of the river, Malá Strana, and the castle is from the tip of Novotného lávka, by the statue of Smetana.

View over Malá Strana

THE NEW TOWN

Finish your beer or coffee in one of the cafés by the Smetana statue and go through the arcade leading to Knights of the Cross Square at the Old Town end of Charles Bridge. Continue in the same direction, then cross the Vltava by the restored Mánes Bridge (Mánesův most). Head for Malostranská Metro station and walk through what is probably the only subway garden in the world to palace-lined Valdštejnská Street, with its unusual close-up view of the castle high above. Tomášská Street leads into Malá Strana Square. Return to the Smetana statue down Mostecká Street and across Charles Bridge, which is particularly enchanting at night.

ORGANIZED TOURS

There are plenty of general tours of the city, as well as more detailed explorations of particular districts and trips that venture out into the surroundings. The difficulty lies in choosing among them, but the best advice is to shop around and consider all the alternatives on offer.

PRAGUE INFORMATION SERVICE

A good starting point for finding out about organized tours is the official Prague Information Service (Pražská informační služba – PIS), at: ✉ Na příkopě 20, Nové město ☎ 54 44 44 or 187 🕐 Winter Mon–Fri 9–6; Sat 9–3. Summer Mon–Fri 9–7; Sat–Sun 9–5 🚇 Náměstí Republiky; or ✉ Můstek or Staroměstské náměstí 1 (Old Town Hall) ☎ 54 44 44 or 187 🕐 Winter Mon–Fri 9–6; Sat–Sun 9–5. Summer Mon–Fri 9–7; Sat–Sun 9–6 🚇 Staroměstská or Můstek. PIS also runs its own tours in a reliable way.

MAIN TOUR OPERATORS

Čedok (the longest-established travel company of all) is at: ✉ Na příkopě 18, Nové město ☎ 2419 7111; fax 2422 3479 🚇 Náměstí Republiky or Můstek; ✉ Pařížská 6, Staré město ☎ 231 6978; fax 232 17 28 🚇 Staroměstská; and ✉ Rytířská 16, Staré město ☎ 26 37 97; fax 26 27 96 🚇 Můstek or Staroměstská.

Premiant City Tour is at: ✉ Na příkopě 23, Nové město ☎ 0601 21 26 25 (mobile).

WALKING TOURS

A main starting point for themed walks downtown is Old Town Square; check local posters for starting times. Also try Prague Walks on Wenceslas Square ✉ Václavské náměstí 60 ☎ 61 21 46 03.

BOAT TOURS

Boat tours along the Vltava range from short, hour-long trips to long excursions that include lunch or dinner.

EVD ➕ E3 ✉ Quayside at Na Františku (near the southern end of Čechův most) ☎ 23 10 208/23 11 915 🚇 Staroměstská.

PPS ➕ D5 ✉ Rašinova nábřeží (south of Jiráskův most) ☎ 29 38 09/29 83 09 🚇 Karlovo náměsti.

Castle tour

A stroll around the castle in the company of a well-informed guide can be instructive. Tours start from the Information Center of Prague Castle in the Third Courtyard (➕ C4 ✉ Hradčany ☎ 2437 3368).

View across the River Vltava to Prague Castle

EXCURSIONS

Karlštejn Castle

INFORMATION

Karlštejn Castle

✉ Hrad Karlštejn

☎ 0311 68 46 17

⏰ Jan–Mar, Nov–Dec Tue–Sun
9–12, 1–4. Apr–Oct
Tue–Sun 9–12, 1–5.
May–Jun, Sep Tue–Sun
9–12, 12:30–6. Jul–Aug
Tue–Sun 9–12, 12:30–7

🚆 Suburban trains from
Prague-Smíchov to Karlštejn:
travel time 40 min

Mělník Castle

✉ Svatováclavská, Mělník

☎ 0206 62 21 21

⏰ Mar–Dec daily 10–5

🚌 Bus from Florenc
bus station: travel time
50 min

KARLŠTEJN CASTLE (HRAD KARLŠTEJN)

This mighty fortress, one of the great sights of Bohemia, towers above the glorious woodlands of the gorge of the River Berounka. There's no motor transportation up from the riverside village, but the superb panorama from the castle walls will fully compensate you for the long climb up. The name of the castle, which was started in 1348, celebrates the Emperor Charles IV. He conceived it as a sort of sacred bunker, a repository for the Crown Jewels and his collection of holy relics. Not merely a fortress, the castle was also planned as a personal, processional way that the emperor would follow to its climax—the Great Tower containing the Chapel of the Holy Rood, reached only after much prayer and contemplation. This gorgeous chamber has had to be sealed off from the public, whose breath was destroying its exquisite artifacts.

MĚLNÍK

Built on a bluff near the confluence of the Vltava and Elbe rivers, this ancient town is famous for the vineyards that rise up in terraces beneath its imposing castle. Following the demise of Communism, Mělník's castle and estates have been returned to the original aristocratic Lobkovic owners. Long before the Lobkovic family, however, it was a royal seat, the abode of the Czech queens, one of whom raised her grandson Wenceslas (later the "Good King") here. The castle courtyard, with its Gothic and Renaissance wings and ancient wine cellars, is approached via the charmingly arcaded town square.

LIDICE

Nowhere could seem more ordinary than this modern little mining village in the dull countryside just beyond Prague airport. But on June 10, 1942, on the flimsiest of pretexts, its male population was shot and its women and children

St. Peter and St. Paul Church, Mělník Castle

sent off to a concentration camp—and Lidice's name resounded round the world as a synonym for Czech suffering and German ruthlessness. Days before, Reichsprotektor Heydrich had been assassinated, and the Nazis needed revenge. Lidice was razed to the ground and its name removed from the records "forever." After the war the village was rebuilt a short distance away, while the site of the atrocity became a memorial museum and park.

KONOPIŠTĚ CASTLE
(ZÁMEK KONOPIŠTĚ)

Konopiště Castle's round towers rise in romantic fashion above the surrounding woodlands. The palace's origins go back to the 14th century, but it owes its present appearance largely to Archduke Franz Ferdinand, heir to the Habsburg throne, who acquired it in 1887. The corridors are filled with trophies of the countless wild creatures he slaughtered while waiting for the demise of his long-lived uncle Franz Josef. The archduke met his own violent end when he was cut down by an assassin's bullet in Sarajevo, thereby triggering the start of World War I. The castle is full of Franz Ferdinand's fine furniture and his extraordinary collection of weapons. His other obsession was landscape gardening, and the splendid parklands and rose garden are a delight.

INFORMATION

Lidice

✉ Monument: 10 cervna 1942, Lidice

☎ 0312 92 33 52

🕓 Jan–Mar, Nov–Dec daily 9–3. Apr–Oct daily 8–5

🚌 Bus from Dejvická Metro stop

Konopiště Castle

✉ Zámek Konopiště, Benesov u Prahy

☎ 0301 213 66

🕓 Apr, Oct Tue–Sun 9–12, 1–3. May–Aug Tue–Sun 9–12, 1–5. Sep Tue–Sun 9–12, 1–4

🚉 Train to Benesov (1 hr) then bus or taxi

WHAT'S ON

MAY/JUNE — *Prague Spring Music Festival* (mid-May): This internationally important event consists of an array of concerts of classical music in churches, palaces, and halls. It starts off with a procession from Smetana's grave in the National Cemetery in Vyšehrad to the great hall named after him in the recently restored Municipal House, where a rousing performance of his orchestral tone poem *Ma Vlast* ("*My Country*") is given

JUNE — *Dance Prague*: An international dance festival with events at various venues, including some public outdoor spaces

OCTOBER — *Mozart Festival*: The cultural program for the month includes even more than the usual Prague allowance of the maestro's masterworks

DECEMBER — *St. Nicholas* (December 5): The streets are roamed by a multitude of St. Nicks, each accompanied by an angel (who rewards good children with candy) and a devil (who chastises appropriately)

Christmas Eve (December 24): Live carp are sold on the streets for the traditional Czech Christmas Eve dinner

New Year's Eve (December 31): Those wanting to celebrate more formally attend "Sylvester" balls, while others welcome the arrival of the New Year on the streets

TICKETS

Tickets for events can be obtained at individual box offices (which may be cheaper) or through:

Prague Information Service ✉ Na příkopě 20, Nové město ☎ 26 40 20 or ✉ Old Town Hall ☎ 24 48 20 18; and

Ticketpro ✉ Salvátorská 10, Staré město ☎ 24 81 40 20.

ENTERTAINMENT INFORMATION

The best source of information for English readers about what's on is probably the tabloid "Night and Day" section of the weekly newspaper *Prague Post*. This gives listings of stage, screen, and cultural events likely to be relevant to visitors from abroad, as well as interesting comment and analysis. A comprehensive review of upcoming events is contained in *Cultural Events*, published monthly by the Prague Information Service.

PRAGUE's
top 25 sights

The sights are shown on the maps on the inside front cover and inside
back cover, numbered **1–25** from west to east across the city

STRAHOV MONASTERY

HIGHLIGHTS

- 17th-century Theological Hall
- 18th-century Philosophical Hall
- Strahov Picture Gallery (Strahovská obrazárna)
- 9th-century Strahov Gospels
- Interior of Church of the Assumption

INFORMATION

- C4
- Strahovské nádvoří 1, Hradčany
- 2051 6671
- Daily 9–12, 1–5
- Peklo (Hell) restaurant in monastery cellars
- Tram 22 to Pohořelec
- Fair
- Moderate
- Loretto Shrine (➤ 26), Petřin Hill (➤ 28)

Baroque spires rising toward Heaven, a gilded image of an enemy of the Faith, monks profiting from an enterprise in Hell: this hilltop monastery (Strahovský klášter) seems to encapsulate this most paradoxical of cities.

Persuasive priests The Strahov Monastery, a major landmark in the cityscape, crowns the steep slope leading up from Malá Strana (its name derives from *strahovní*, meaning "to watch over"). It is a treasure house of literature, and its ornate library halls with their splendid frescoes are among the most magnificent in Europe. As befits a monastery devoted to books, Strahov owed much to its abbots' way with words. Its 12th-century founder, Abbot Zdík, persuaded Prince Vladislav II to back his project by making flattering comparisons of Prague with the holy city of Jerusalem. Much later, in 1783, Abbot Meyer exercised equal powers of persuasion on Emperor Joseph II to exempt Strahov from the reforming ruler's edict that closed down many of the Habsburg Empire's monasteries. The canny cleric was so eloquent that Strahov actually benefited from the misfortune of other institutions: books from the suppressed monastery at Louka were brought here by the wagonload. A gilded medallion of the emperor over the library entrance may also have helped to persuade Joseph that the Strahov monks deserved special treatment.

Returnees' revenge The monks, who belong to the Premonstratensian Order, were chased out of Strahov by the Communists in 1952, but have now come back. They have made the upper floor of the cloisters into a gallery for the works of art since returned to them and converted the cellars into a restaurant called Hell (Peklo).

NOVÝ SVĚT

Chambermaids and scullions, footmen and flunkies, these were the folk for whom the humble homes of Nový Svět ("New World") were originally erected back in the 14th century. The area is now more upscale.

Wizards and weird doings Nový Svět, a mysterious place of crooked alleyways and secret gardens hidden behind high walls, has never been in the city's mainstream. Aside from the castle servants, those able to cater for the more esoteric interests of their masters came here. They included the Danish astronomer Tycho Brahe and his German colleague Johannes Kepler, both employed by Rudolph II to investigate the more arcane secrets of the universe.

La Bohème Today's residents are artists and writers, who have colonized the pretty 18th-century houses along this charming cobbled street that wobbles its way westward just uphill from the castle. The painter's studio at No. 19 is crammed with pictures of curvaceous girls and grimacing gnomes, while the Czech master of animated film, Jan Švankmajer, a long-time resident, runs a gallery devoted to Surrealist art.

Connecting the worlds "New World" is linked to the outside world by short streets (Loretánská, Kapucínská, U Kasáren, and Kanovnická) that run down the hill from the main tourist trail between the Strahov Monastery and the castle, or by flights of steps that lead from the old ramparts (whose course is followed by today's tram No. 22).

HIGHLIGHTS

- Nepomuk statue in Černinská Street
- Birthplace of violinist F. Ondříček at No. 25
- Tycho Brahe's house at No. 1
- Church of St. John Nepomuk
- No. 3, the president's favorite restaurant

INFORMATION

- ✚ C4
- ✉ Nový Svět, Hradčany
- 🍴 Restaurant at No. 3
- 🚊 Tram 22 to Brusnice
- ♿ Few
- ↔ Loretto Shrine (➤ 26)

St. John Nepomuk

LORETTO SHRINE

HIGHLIGHTS

- The main façade, with statuary and carillon
- The Santa Casa
- Interior of the Church of the Nativity
- Diamond monstrance in the Loretto Treasure
- Cloister painting of St. Starosta

Loretto Shrine, Hradčany

INFORMATION

✚ C4

✉ Loretánské náměstí, Hradčany

☎ 2051 6740

🕐 Tue–Sun 9–12:15, 1–4:30

🚌 Tram 22 to Pohořelec

♿ None

▥ Moderate

↔ Strahov Monastery (➤ 24), Nový Svět (➤ 25)

A bearded lady, skeletons rattling their bones to the sound of chiming bells, severed breasts on display, a flying house: these are not part of a freak show, but instead are all features of the sumptuous Loretto Shrine (Loreta), high up on Hradčany Hill.

Counter-Reformation fireworks No showman's trick was spared to bring the wayward Czechs back into the Catholic fold after their long flirtation with Protestantism was brought to an end by the Battle of the White Mountain in 1620. Protestant austerity, with its dislike of images, was replaced by the idolatry of the cult of the Virgin Mary, dripping with sensuality and symbolism. Of all the flights of architectural fantasy that the Roman Catholic Counter-Reformation perpetrated on Prague, the Loretto is the most bizarre as well as the most beautiful, its church and courtyard a theater of cults, miracles, and mysteries designed to dazzle doubters and skeptics.

Weird wonders The kernel of the complex is a Santa Casa, a facsimile of the Virgin Mary's holy home in Nazareth, supposedly flown by angels from the Holy Land and deposited at Loreta in Italy. Fifty such shrines were once scattered around the Czech countryside, but this is far and away the most important, an ornate little Renaissance pavilion built in 1631 and later given an equally ornate Baroque setting of courtyard, carillon tower, and richly decorated church. Pilgrims once flocked here in huge numbers to marvel at the macabre: St. Agatha offering up her bloody bosom to the angels; the skeletons in their wax death masks; unhappy St. Starosta, whose father killed her in a fury on finding she'd grown a beard to discourage a favored suitor.

ŠTERNBERG PALACE

Who would guess that the unpretentious little alley beside the Prague archbishop's palace on Hradčany Square would lead to one of the Continent's great art collections? Housed in the Šternberg Palace (Šternberský palác), it dazzles visitors with its Old Masters and modern works.

Ambitious aristocrats Having built the Troja Château (► 48) on the edge of Prague, Count Šternberg, one of the city's richest men, needed a town house closer to Prague Castle. The Italian architect Giovanni Alliprandi was commissioned to design the palace, and work began on the count's Hradčany home in 1698. However, the money ran out before the main façade (the principal purpose of which was to upstage his neighbor, the archbishop) could be completed. The interior was decorated with fine ceiling and wall paintings. It was a later Šternberg who donated much of the family's great picture collection to the fledgling National Gallery in the early 19th century, and the nation's finest foreign paintings were housed here from 1814 to 1871. They are once more in this grand setting.

Picture palace Despite being tucked away behind Hradčany Square, the Šternberg Palace is an edifice of some substance, arranged around an imposing courtyard, with grand stairways and an oval pavilion facing the garden. The National Gallery of European Art attracts a stream of tourists—as well as art thieves, tempted (until it was tightened up not long ago) by laughably lax security. The pictures could keep an art lover busy for a whole day or more, though some star exhibits are no longer on view: "Restitution" has returned them to the owners from whom they were confiscated by the Communists.

HIGHLIGHTS

- Triptych of the *Adoration of the Magi,* Giertgen tot Sint Jans
- *Adam and Eve,* Cranach
- *Feast of the Rosary,* Dürer
- *Scholar in his Study,* Rembrandt
- *Head of Christ,* El Greco
- Icons from 2nd-century Egypt
- *Beheading of St. Dorothy,* Hans Baldung Grien
- *Martyrdom of St. Florian,* Altdorfer
- *St. Jerome,* Ribera
- *The Thames,* Canaletto

INFORMATION

- ✚ C4
- ✉ Hradčanské náměstí 15, Hradčany
- ☎ 2051 4595
- 🕐 Tue–Sun 10–6
- 🚊 Tram 22 to Pražský hrad
- ♿ Few
- 🚹 Moderate
- ↔ Prague Castle (► 29), Military Museum, Schwarzenberg Palace (► 53)

Top: Melancholie II, *Jan Zrzavý*

PETŘÍN HILL

When the press of the crowd on Charles Bridge becomes too much and the sidewalks become too hard, there's always the glorious green of the Petřín, its orchards and woodlands a cool retreat from the city center.

HIGHLIGHTS

- Rozhledna—viewing tower
- 14th-century Hunger Wall
- Mirror Maze (Bludiště)
- Charles Bridge Battle diorama
- Observatory and Planetarium
- Rose Garden
- Alpine Garden
- Baroque Church of St. Lawrence
- Calvary Chapel and Stations of the Cross
- Ukrainian timber Church of St. Michael

INFORMATION

- ✚ C–D4–5
- 🕑 Rozhledna: Apr–Aug daily 10–7. Sep–Oct daily 10–6. Nov–Mar Sat–Sun 10–5. Mirror Maze: Apr–Aug daily 10–7. Sep–Nov Mon–Fri 10–5; Sat–Sun 10–6. Nov–Mar Sat–Sun 10–5. Observatory: hours vary; for information call PIS on ☎ 54 44 44 or 187
- 🍴 Restaurant and café
- 🚊 Tram 22 to Strahov then walk
- 🚠 Funicular railway, Újezd in Malá Strana
- ♿ Few
- 💰 Rozhledna, Mirror Maze, Observatory: moderate
- ↔ Strahov Monastery (➤ 24)

A train with a view In 1891, for the city's great Jubilee Expo that celebrated the achievements of the Czech provinces when they still formed part of the Austrian Empire, the city fathers provided a jolly little funicular railway (the "Lanovka") to the top of Petřín Hill. Now restored, it once again carries passengers effortlessly up and down the steep slope. At the top there's a whole array of attractions, including the Rozhledna ("Lookout"), the little brother of the Eiffel Tower, also built in 1891. Its 299 steps lead to a viewing platform; some claim to have seen, on a clear day, not only the Czech Republic's Giant Mountains (90 miles to the northeast) but also the Alps (even farther away to the southwest). And all of Prague is at your feet.

Country matters With its woods and orchards (splendid with blossom in spring), the Petřín brings a real breath of the countryside into the metropolis and provides a counterpoint to the busy castle area. Once there were vineyards on the hill, but these didn't survive the Thirty Years War, and were replaced by the superb gardens that link the palaces of Malá Strana to the surrounding hillside parklands.

Rozhledna tower, Petřín

PRAGUE CASTLE

The thousand windows of Pražský hrad (Prague Castle) gaze down into every corner of the city. This is the citadel of the Czech nation, the holder of its collective memory. It is a place of palaces, churches, streets, squares, and alleyways, a city within a city, sheltering the homes of some of the country's greatest treasures.

Age-old stronghold The princes of Prague first built a fortress on the limestone spur high above the Vltava in the 9th century, and the Czech provinces have been ruled from here ever since (except when rulers preferred to live in a long-vanished palace downtown or on the summit of the rock upstream at Vyšehrad). Every age has left its imprint on the castle; it is a storehouse of architectural styles, ranging from the foundations of Romanesque churches a thousand years old to Professor Plečnik's premature Post-modernism of the interwar years. Even now, a committee is hard at work adapting the ancient complex in an attempt to make it more inviting and accessible to the citizens of a new and democratic order.

Castle denizens Teeming with tourists, the castle's courtyards also echo with the tread of countless ghosts: Emperor Charles IV, with his dreams of Prague as a great imperial capital; the cranky Habsburg ruler Rudolph II, attended by his retinue of alchemists and necromancers, soothsayers, and erotic painters; the Protestant mob that flung the hated Catholic councellors down from the Chancellery windows; Tomáš Masaryk, philosopher-president and creator of Czechoslavakia; Adolf Hitler *Heil*-ing his hysterical helots; and, most recently, the Communists, enjoying their privileges while they lasted.

HIGHLIGHTS

- Giants guarding western gateway
- Mihulka (Powder Tower)
- Vladislav Hall in Old Royal Palace
- Tiny houses in Golden Lane
- Lobkovic Palace (History Museum)
- Outline of Matthias Gate in First Courtyard
- Second Courtyard, with Holy Rood Chapel
- Third Courtyard, with statue of St. George
- Plečnik's canopy and stairway to gardens
- Riders' Staircase in Old Royal Palace

INFORMATION

- ✚ C–D4
- ✉ Pražský hrad, Hradčany
- ☎ 2437 3368
- ◷ Courtyards and streets: daily until late. Buildings: Apr–Oct Tue–Sun 9–5. Nov–Mar Tue–Sun 9–4
- 🍴 Cafés and restaurants
- 🚃 Tram 22 to Pražský hrad
- ♿ Few
- 🎫 Moderate
- ↔ Šternberg Palace (► 27), St. Vitus's Cathedral (► 30)

ST. VITUS'S CATHEDRAL

HIGHLIGHTS

- South Portal, with 14th-century mosaic
- St. Wenceslas's Chapel
- Crypt, with royal tombs
- Silver tomb of St. John Nepomuk
- West front sculptures

INFORMATION

- C/D4
- Pražský hrad, Hradčany
- Apr–Oct daily 9–5.
  Nov–Mar daily 9–4. Tower:
  Apr–Oct daily 10–5
- Restaurants and cafés in castle
- Tram 22 to Pražský hrad
- Few
- Prague Castle (➤ 29)

Tomb of St. John Nepomuk

To emerge into Prague Castle's Third Courtyard and see the twin towers of St. Vitus's Cathedral (katedrála svatého Víta) lancing skyward is truly breathtaking. The sight is all the more compelling when you realize that this Gothic edifice was completed within living memory.

Spanning the centuries The cathedral was begun by Emperor Charles IV in the middle of the 14th century. It is built over the foundations of much earlier predecessors: a round church erected by "Good King" Wenceslas in the early 10th century and a big Romanesque building resembling the present-day St. George's Basilica (➤ 31). The glory of the architecture is largely due to the great Swabian builder Petr Parléř and his sons, who worked on the building for some 60 years. Progress was halted abruptly by the troubles of the 15th century, and the cathedral consisted only of an east end until the formation of an "Association for the Completion of the Cathedral," in 1843. Decades of effort saw the nave, western towers, and much else brought to a triumphant conclusion; in 1929, a thousand years after King Wenceslas was assassinated, the cathedral was consecrated, dedicated to the country's patron saint, St. Vitus.

Cathedral treasures The cathedral is a treasure house of Bohemian history, though the Crown Jewels, its greatest prize, are seldom on display. The spacious interior absorbs the crowds with ease and provides a fitting context for an array of precious artifacts that ranges from medieval paintings to modern glass.

St. George's Basilica & Convent

A bull's-blood-colored Baroque façade conceals a severe ancient interior, the Romanesque Basilica of St. George (Bazilika a Klášter sv Jiří). The nuns have long since left their convent to the north, now a worthy setting for fine collections of Gothic, Renaissance, and Baroque painting and sculpture.

Bare basilica The basilica is the biggest church of its date in the Czech provinces, its twin towers and pale, sober stonework a reminder of the great antiquity of the castle complex. Very well preserved, it is no longer a church but is now a concert venue, and the austere interior, a great hall with wooden ceiling, houses a small number of impressive artworks.

Paintings and princesses Founded in 973, St. George's Convent was a prestigious institution, a place to which princesses and other young ladies of noble birth were sent to receive the best possible education. Shut down like many other religious houses in 1782 by Emperor Joseph (who turned it into a barracks), it had to await the coming of the Communists for its rehabilitation; they planned to turn it into a Museum of the Czechoslovak People. A painfully long period of restoration has provided a more than adequate home for one of the country's greatest and most distinctive galleries, the National Gallery of Old Bohemian Art. In the Middle Ages, artists from Bohemia led Europe in their ability to convey the serene beauty of undisturbed faith; their sculpture and painting, displayed in the atmospheric setting of the convent's cellars, is unsurpassed. The upper floors contain the work of Prague's equally creative Renaissance and Baroque periods.

HIGHLIGHTS

- Sculpture of *St. George and the Dragon*
- Krumlov's *Madonna and Child* sculpture
- Painted panels by the Master of Vyšší Brod
- Portraits of saints by Master Theodorik
- *Christ on the Mount of Olives* by the Třeboň Master
- Tympanum from Týn Church in Old Town
- Statue of Hercules
- *Tobias Restoring his Father's Sight* by Petr Brandl
- Landscapes by Roland Savary
- Genre scenes by Norbert Grund

INFORMATION

- ➕ D4
- ✉ Jiřské náměstí, Hradčany
- ☎ 5732 0536
- 🕐 Tue–Sun 10–6
- 🍴 Restaurants and cafés in castle
- Ⓜ Malostranská, then an uphill walk
- 🚊 Tram 22 to Pražský hrad
- ♿ Few
- 🎟 Moderate
- ↔ Prague Castle (➤ 29)

NERUDA STREET

Toil up to the castle from Malá Strana Square via steep, cobbled Neruda Street (Nerudova), and you will be rewarded by a sequence of exquisite town houses, Baroque and rococo, on medieval foundations. Most have elaborate house signs.

Eagles and other emblems It is the elegant façades and their emblems that catch the eye. There's an Eagle, Three Little Fiddles, a Goblet, a Golden Key, and a Horseshoe. The Two Suns indicate the house (No. 47) of author Jan Neruda (1843–1891), who gave his name to the street; he was the Dickens of Malá Strana, a shrewd observer of the everyday life of the area. Most of the people who lived here were prosperous burghers, but there were some aristocrats, like the Morzins who built their palace at No. 5 (the muscular Moors holding up the balcony are a pun on the family name). Their home is now an embassy, as is the Thun-Hohensteins' palace at No. 20; here the Moors' job is being carried out by a pair of odd-looking eagles.

Spur Street The secret of savoring Neruda Street to the full is to coast gently downward, like the coachmen from whom the road derived its earlier German name of Spornergasse (Spur Street), the spur in this case being the skid-like brake that slowed their otherwise precipitous progress down the steep slope.

HIGHLIGHTS

- No. 2, U kocoura (The Tomcat) pub
- No. 5, Morzin Palace
- No. 6, The Red Eagle
- No. 12, The Three Little Fiddles
- No. 16, The Golden Goblet
- No. 20, Thun-Hohenstein Palace
- No. 27, The Golden Key
- No. 34, The Golden Horseshoe
- Baroque Church of Our Lady of Divine Providence
- No. 47, The Two Suns, home of Jan Neruda

INFORMATION

- ✚ C–D4
- ✉ Nerudova, Malá Strana
- 🍴 Restaurants and cafés
- 🚊 Tram 22 to Malá Strana Square (Malostranské náměstí)
- ♿ Few
- ↔ Prague Castle (▶ 29), St. Nicholas's Church, Malá Strana (▶ 33)

The Three Little Fiddles, No. 12 Nerudova

St. Nicholas's Church, Malá Strana

As you crawl insect-like around the base of this cliff of a church you feel the full power of the Catholic Counter-Reformation expressing itself in what is surely one of the boldest and most beautiful Baroque buildings of Central Europe.

Counter-Reformation citadel When the Jesuits came to Prague following the rout of the Protestants at the Battle of the White Mountain, the existing little 13th century church at the center of Malá Strana Square was far too modest for their aspirations. The new St. Nicholas's Church (Chrám svatého Mikuláše) was eventually completed in the 18th century and, with its lofty walls and high dome and bell tower, became one of the dominant features of the city. The Jesuits intended their church to impress, but not through size alone. They employed the finest architects of the day (the Dientzenhofers, father and son, plus Anselmo Lurago), along with the most talented interior designers. The subtly undulating west front is adorned with statues proclaiming the triumph of the Jesuit Order under the patronage of the imperial House of Habsburg. Inside, no effort was spared to enthrall via the dynamic play of space, statuary, and painting, a fantastically decorated pulpit, and a 2,500-pipe organ (played by Mozart on several occasions).

Princely palaces and humbler households In front of the church swirls the life of Malá Strana, locals waiting for the trams mixing with tourists following the Royal Way (▶16). Malá Strana Square is lined with a fascinating mixture of ancient town houses and grand palaces, while attached to St. Nicholas's is the Jesuits' college, now part of the university.

HIGHLIGHTS

St. Nicholas's Church
- West front
- St. Barbara's Chapel
- Organ with fresco of St. Cecilia
- Dome with Holy Trinity fresco
- Huge sculptures of four Church Fathers
- Trompe-l'oeil ceiling fresco by Krackor

Malá Strana Square
- Arcaded houses
- No. 10, Renaissance house
- No. 13, Liechtenstein Palace of 1791
- Nos. 18 and 19, Smiřický Palace and Šternberg House

INFORMATION

- ⊞ D4
- ✉ Malostranské náměstí
- 🕐 Apr–Sep daily 9–5. Oct–Mar daily 9–4:30
- 🍴 Restaurants and cafés in square
- Ⓜ Malostranská
- 🚃 Tram 12, 22 to Malostranské náměstí
- ♿ Few
- 💲 Inexpensive
- ↔ Neruda Street (▶32), Wallenstein Palace (▶34), Charles Bridge (▶35)

WALLENSTEIN PALACE

- Sala Terrena
- Garden sculptures (copies of originals by de Vries)
- Grotesquery and aviary in garden
- Riding School (museum with temporary exhibitions)

INFORMATION

- ✚ D4
- ✉ Valdštejnské náměstí, Malá Strana
- ◎ Palace: closed to public. Garden: May–Oct
- Ⓜ Malostranská
- ♿ Few
- 🎟 Free
- ↔ Neruda Street (▶ 32), St. Nicholas's Church, Malá Strana (▶ 33)

Think of this palace—Prague's biggest—as an awful warning, an admonition to eschew excessive ambition and arrogance of the kind shown by its builder, Albrecht von Wallenstein, whose aspirations to power and fame led to his assassination.

Greedy generalissimo Wallenstein's huge late Renaissance/early Baroque palace (Valdštejnský palác) crouches at the foot of Prague Castle as if waiting to gobble it up. A whole city block, previously occupied by a couple of dozen houses and a brickworks, was demolished to make way for the complex of five courtyards, a barracks, a riding school, and a superb garden that were intended to reflect Wallenstein's wealth and status. Wallenstein (Valdštejn in Czech) turned the troubled early 17th century to his advantage. Having wormed his way into the emperor's favor, he became governor of Prague, then duke of Friedland. He married for money (twice), and great tracts of land (even whole towns) fell into his hands following the Battle of the White Mountain in 1620. His fortunes grew further as he quartermastered the imperial armies as well as leading them. Rightly suspicious of his subject's intentions—Wallenstein was negotiating with the enemy—the emperor had him killed.

The general's garden The great hall of the palace, with its ceiling painting of Wallenstein as Mars, the god of war, can only be seen if you have friends in the Czech Senate, which now occupies the building. The formal garden is more freely accessible. The latter is dominated by the superb Sala Terrena loggia, modeled on those in Italy, and has convincing copies of the statues stolen by Swedish soldiers during the Thirty Years War.

CHARLES BRIDGE

Any time is right for a visit to Prague's magnificent medieval bridge over the River Vltava. Enjoy the antics of the hucksters, then return to savor the almost sinister atmosphere of dusk, when the sculpted saints along the parapets gesticulate against the darkening sky.

Gothic overpass For centuries this was Prague's only bridge, built on the orders of Emperor Charles IV in the 14th century. It's a triumph of Gothic engineering, 16 massive sandstone arches carrying it more than 1,600 feet from the Old Town to soar across Kampa Island and the Vltava River to touch down almost in the heart of Malá Strana. It is protected by sturdy timber cutwaters and guarded at both ends by towers; the eastern face of the Old Town Bridge Tower is richly ornamented. Its opposite number is accompanied by a smaller tower, once part of the earlier Judith Bridge.

Starry saint Charles Bridge has always been much more than a river crossing. Today's traders succeed earlier merchants and stallholders, and tournaments, battles, and executions have all been held on the bridge. The heads of the Protestants executed in 1621 in Old Town Square were displayed here. Later that century the bridge was beautified with Baroque sculptures, including the statue of St. John Nepomuk. Falling foul of the king, this unfortunate cleric was pushed off the bridge in a sack. As his body bobbed in the water, five stars danced on the surface. Nepomuk hence became the patron saint of bridges, and is always depicted with his starry halo.

HIGHLIGHTS

- Old Town Bridge Tower
- Malá Strana Bridge Tower (viewpoint)
- Nepomuk statue with bronze relief panels
- Bruncvík (Roland column) to southwest
- Statue of St. John of Matha
- Bronze crucifix with Hebrew inscription
- Statue of St. Luitgard (by Braun)

INFORMATION

- D4
- Staroměstská
- Tram 12, 22 to Malá Strana Square
- Good
- St. Nicholas's Church, Malá Strana (➤ 33)

St. Anthony of Padua

NATIONAL THEATER

HIGHLIGHTS

- Bronze troikas above the entrance loggia
- Star-patterned roof of the dome
- Frescoes in the foyer by Mikóláš Aleš
- Painted ceiling of the auditorium, by František Ženíšek
- Painted stage curtain by Vojtěch Hynais
- View of the theater from Střelecký Island
- Any performance of an opera from the Czech repertoire

INFORMATION

- ✚ D/E5
- ✉ Národní 2, Nové město
- ☎ 24 91 34 37
- ⏹ Bar
- Ⓠ Národní třída
- ♿ Few
- ↔ Bethlehem Chapel (➤ 55)

The National Theater reflected in the Vltava

Even if the thought of a classical play performed in Czech doesn't enthrall you, don't miss the National Theater (Národní divadlo). It is, perhaps, the greatest of Prague's collective works of art, decorated by the finest artists of the age.

National drama In the mid-19th century, theater in Prague still spoke with a German voice. Money to build a specifically Czech theater was collected from 1849 onward, without support from German-dominated officialdom. The foundation stone was laid in 1868 with much festivity, then in 1881, just before the first performance, the whole place burned down. Undiscouraged, the populace rallied, and by 1893 the theater had been completely rebuilt. The opening was celebrated with a grand gala performance of the opera *Libuše* by Smetana, a passionate supporter of the theater project.

Expanded ambition The National Theater stands at the New Town end of the Legions Bridge (most Legií), its bulk carefully angled to fit into the streetscape and not diminish the view to Petřín Hill on the far bank. It was given a long-deserved restoration in time for its centenary, and when it reopened in 1983 it had gained a piazza and three annexes, whose architecture has been much maligned, the least unkind comment being that the buildings seem to be clad in bubble-wrap. Prague's well-known Laterna Magika multimedia show performs in one of these additional buildings, the Nova scéna.

14

DECORATIVE ARTS MUSEUM

Don't be put off by the uninviting building or the forlornly flapping banner that proclaims the museum's name (Uměleckoprůmyslové muzeum). At the top of a steep flight of stairs are little-visited treasure chambers full of fine furniture, glass, porcelain, clocks, metalwork, and more.

Riverside reclaimed Looking something like a miniature Louvre, the museum was built in 1901 in an area that, by the end of the 19th century, had turned its back on the river and had become a jumble of storage depots and timber yards. The city fathers determined to beautify it with fine public buildings and riverside promenades on the Parisian model. The School of Arts and Crafts (1884) and the House of Artists (1890) preceded the Decorative Arts Museum; the University's Philosophy Building (1929), which completed the enclosure of what is now Jan Palach Square, followed it.

Decorative delights The museum's collections are incredibly rich and diverse, numbering nearly 200,000 items of international origin. Unfortunately, only a fraction has ever been on display at any one time. The focus is on beautiful objects originating in the Czech provinces and dating from Renaissance times to the 19th century. They are displayed in an endearingly old-fashioned way, in sumptuous settings.

The extraordinary Czech contribution to the development of 20th-century art and design has never been dealt with adequately, a situation that has recently been remedied partly by the opening of the Museum of Modern Art (► 47).

HIGHLIGHTS

- *Pietra dura* scene of a town by Castnicci
- Beer glasses engraved with card players
- Boulle commode and cabinet
- Monumental Baroque furniture by Dientzenhofer and Santini
- Meissen Turk on a rhino
- Holic porcelain figures
- Harrachov glass
- Klášterec figurines of Prague characters
- Biedermeier cradle
- Surprise view down into the Old Jewish Cemetery

INFORMATION

- ✚ E4
- ✉ 17 listopadu 2, Staré město
- ☎ 24 81 12 41
- 🕐 Tue–Sun 10–6
- 🍴 Café (🕐 Mon–Fri 10–6; Sat–Sun 10:30–6)
- Ⓜ Staroměstská
- ♿ Few
- ⚠ Moderate
- ↔ Old/New Synagogue, Josefov (► 39), Old Jewish Cemetery (► 40)

VYŠEHRAD

HIGHLIGHTS

- National Cemetery (Slavín) graves and memorials
- St. Martin's Rotunda (Romanesque church)
- Brick Gate (Cihelná brána), with Prague Fortifications Museum
- Vyšehrad Museum, with historical exhibits
- Baroque Leopold Gate
- Ramparts walk
- Neo-Gothic Church of St. Peter and St. Paul
- Freestanding sculptures of Libuše and other legendary figures (by Josef Václav Myslbek)

INFORMATION

- ✚ E7
- ✉ Museum: Soběslavova 1, Vyšehrad
- ☎ Museum: 29 66 51
- ◷ Museum: Apr–Oct daily 9:30–5:30. Nov–Mar daily 9:30–4:30. Cemetery: Jan–Feb, Nov–Dec daily 9–4. Mar–Apr, Oct daily 8–6. May–Sep daily 8–7
- 🍴 Cafés
- Ⓜ Vyšehrad
- ♿ Few
- 🎫 Park: free. Museum and cemetery: inexpensive
- ↔ Palace of Culture, Vyšehrad (► 51)

Rising high above the River Vltava is Vyšehrad ("High Castle"), where the sooth-saying Princess Libuše foresaw the founding of Prague, "a city whose splendor shall reach unto the stars," and where she married her plowman swain, Přemysl.

Romantic rock Beneath Vyšehrad's 19th-century neo-Gothic Church of St. Peter and St. Paul are the remains of a far earlier, Romanesque church that once served the royal court. But it was in the 19th century, with the rise of Romantic ideas about history and nationhood, that poets, playwrights, and painters celebrated the great fortress-rock, elaborating the story of Libuše. Most of their efforts have been forgotten, though Smetana's "Vyšehrad," part of his glorious tone-poem *Má vlast*, is still popular. The nation's great and

Devil's Pillars, Karlach's Park

good have been buried in the Slavín, the National Cemetery (or Pantheon) at Vyšehrad, since the late 19th century. Smetana himself is here, along with fellow-composer Dvořák.

Vltava views Everyone driving along the main riverside highway has to pay homage to Vyšehrad, as the road and tram tracks twist and turn and then tunnel through the high rock protruding into the Vltava. In the 1920s the whole hilltop was turned into a public park, with wonderful views up and down the river (► 51).

OLD/NEW SYNAGOGUE, JOSEFOV

To step down from the street through the low portal of Josefov's Old/New Synagogue (Staronová synagóga) is to enter another world, one that endured a thousand years until brought to a tragic end by Nazi occupation.

Ghetto memories The Old/New Synagogue stands at the heart of Josefov, the former Jewish Ghetto. Prague's Jews moved here in the 13th century; by that time they had already lived at various locations in the city for hundreds of years. High walls kept the Jews in and their Christian neighbors out, though not in 1389, when 3,000 Jews died in a vicious pogrom and the synagogue's floor ran with blood. The ghetto community produced some extraordinary characters, such as Rabbi Loew—Renaissance scholar, confidant of emperors, and creator of that archetypal man-made monster, the Golem. Molded from river mud, the mournful Golem first served his master dutifully, but eventually ran amok until the rabbi managed to calm him down. Legend has it that the monster's remains are hidden in the synagogue's loft. Far worse monsters marched in as the Germans annexed Czechoslovakia in 1939; by the end of World War II most of the country's Jews had perished, some in the Czech prison town of Terezín/Theresienstadt, the majority in Auschwitz.

Gothic synagogue With its pointed brick gable and atmospheric interior, the Gothic Old/New Synagogue of 1275 is the oldest building of its kind north of the Alps, a compelling reminder of the age-old intertwining of Jewish and Christian culture in Europe. It is at its most evocative when least crowded with visitors. Remember that for Prague's few remaining Jews it is not a museum but still a place of worship.

HIGHLIGHTS

- Vine carving in entrance portal
- Unconventional five-ribbed vaults
- Gothic grille of the *bimah* (pulpit)
- Rabbi Loew's seat
- Imperial banner recognizing Jewish bravery in the Thirty Years War
- Ark with foliage carving

INFORMATION

- E4
- Pařížská and Červená
- Jan–Mar, Nov–Dec Sun–Thu 9–4:30; Fri 9–2. Apr–Oct Sun–Thu 9–6; Fri 9–5
- Restaurant in Jewish Town Hall
- Staroměstská
- Few
- Moderate
- Decorative Arts Museum (➤ 37), Old Jewish Cemetery (➤ 40), Old Town Square (➤ 42)

OLD JEWISH CEMETERY

HIGHLIGHTS

Around the cemetery
- Jewish Town Hall with Hebraic clock
- Klausen Synagogue (Jewish traditions exhibit)
- Ceremonial Hall
- Pinkas Synagogue (77,297 names of Holocaust victims; pictures from Terezín/ Theresienstadt)
- Statue of Rabbi Loew on New Town Hall, Old Town

In the cemetery
- Tombstone of Rabbi Loew (c. 1525–1609)
- Tombstone of Mayor Maisel (1528–1601)

INFORMATION

- E4
- U starého hřbitova, Staré město
- State Jewish Museum: 231 7191
- Sun–Fri 9–4:30
- Restaurant in Jewish Town Hall
- Staroměstská
- None
- Moderate
- Decorative Arts Museum (➤ 37), Old/New Synagogue, Josefov (➤ 39), Old Town Square (➤ 42)

Just as the sunlight filtering through the tall trees is reduced to a dappled shade, so visitors' voices diminish to a hush as they contemplate the 12,000 toppling tombstones of this ancient burial place (Starý židovský hřbitov).

The changing Ghetto Over the centuries, the Jewish Ghetto, hemmed in by its walls, became intolerably crowded. By the time Emperor Joseph II gave the Jews partial emancipation toward the end of the 18th century, the Ghetto had 12,000 inhabitants, crammed together within it in increasingly sordid conditions. During the course of the 19th century many moved out to more salubrious quarters in the suburbs. Around 1900, the city fathers decided to "improve" the Ghetto, by then named Josefov ("Joseph's Town") in honor of the emperor. Most of it was flattened to make way for broad streets and boulevards, though the rococo Jewish Town Hall and a clutch of synagogues around the cemetery were spared. They survived under the German occupation, because Hitler hoped to preserve what was left of the Ghetto as a "Museum of a Vanished Race." The stolen valuables of the Jewish communities of Bohemia and Moravia were brought to Prague, where some are now on display in the synagogues administered by the State Jewish Museum.

Solemn cemetery The cemetery is evocative of the long centuries of Jewish life in Prague. Unable to extend it, the custodians were forced to bury the dead one on top of the other, up to 12 deep in places. The total number laid to rest here may amount to 80,000. Visitors leave wishful notes under pebbles on the more prominent tombstones (like that of Rabbi Loew).

ST. AGNES'S CONVENT

*A few years ago it seemed unlikely that
the restoration of St. Agnes's Convent
(Anežský klášter) would ever be finished.
However, the city's most venerable Gothic
complex is now open to the public, a fit
setting for a fascinating and unfamiliar
art collection.*

Canonized Czech Agnes was a 13th-century
princess, sister of Wenceslas I and founder of a
convent of Poor Clares here. In its glory days
St. Agnes's was a mausoleum for the royal family,
but was sacked by the Hussites in the 15th century. In 1782, it was closed down by Joseph II,
and for more than a century it became a slum, its
noble interior partitioned and crammed with ten-
ants. At the turn of the century, the convent was
saved from demolition by public protest. It was
another hundred years before it was restored—
by the Communists. On November 12, 1989, just
days before the Communist regime ended,
Agnes was made a saint. An auspicious augury?

National collection The convent now houses
the National Gallery's extensive collections
of 19th-century Czech
art. Watch for works
by Josef Mánes
(painter   and
revolutionary),
Mikóláš   Aleš
(painter   and
graphic artist),
Josef Myslbek
(sculptor and
graphic artist),
and   Jakub
Schikaneder,   a
painter of atmos-
pheric urban scenes.

HIGHLIGHTS

- Rustic idyll *Below the Cottage*, Josef Mánes
- History painting *Oldřich and Božena*, F. Ženíšek
- *Winter Evening in Town*, Jakub Schikaneder
- Study for the Wenceslas statue, Josef Myslbek
- *Primeval Forest*, Julius Mařák
- Vaulted medieval cloister
- Church of St. Francis (concert hall)
- Church of the Holy Savior

INFORMATION

- ✚ E3
- ✉ U milosrdných 17, Staré město
- ☎ 24 81 06 28
- 🅾 Tue–Sun 10–6
- 🍴 Café
- Ⓜ Staroměstská
- 🚋 Tram 17 (Právnická fakulta stop) or Tram 5, 14 (Dlouhá třída stop)
- ♿ Few
- 💷 Moderate
- ↔ Postal Museum (▶ 53)

Below the Cottage,
by *Josef Mánes*   **41**

OLD TOWN SQUARE

HIGHLIGHTS

- Astronomical Clock (Orloj) from the 15th century (► 59)
- Council Hall and Clock Tower (► 50) of Old Town Hall
- Sgraffitoed House at the Minute dated 1611 (No. 2)
- Baroque Church of St. Nicholas
- Jan Hus Memorial of 1915
- Pavement crosses in front of Old Town Hall
- Goltz-Kinský Palace (Graphic Art Collection; ► 52)
- Gothic House at the Stone Bell (► 52)
- Renaissance house (No. 14)
- Arcaded houses Nos. 22–26, with Baroque façades and medieval interiors and cellars

INFORMATION

- ✚ E4
- ✉ Staroměstské náměstí, Staré město
- 🍴 Restaurants and cafés
- 🚊 Staroměstská
- ♿ Fair
- ↔ Old/New Synagogue, Josefov (► 39)

Visitors throng this spacious square (Staroměstské náměstí) at all times of year, entertained by buskers, refreshed at outdoor cafés, and enchanted by the Astronomical Clock and the cheerful façades of the old buildings.

Square and Týn Church

Martyrs and mournful memories The Old Town Square has not always been so jolly. The medieval marketplace, became a scene of execution where Hussites lost their heads in the 15th century and 27 prominent Protestants were put to death in 1621 (they are commemorated by white crosses in the pavement). In 1945, in a final act of spite, diehard Nazis demolished a whole wing of the Old Town Hall; the site has still not been built on. On February 21, 1948, Premier Gottwald proclaimed the triumph of Communism from the rococo Goltz-Kinský Palace.

Round the square The hub of the square is the Jan Hus Memorial, an extraordinary art-nouveau sculpture whose base is one of the few places in the square where you can sit without having to buy a drink! From here, to your left rise the blackened towers of the Týn Church, while to your right is the Old Town Hall, an attractively varied assembly of buildings and, further round, the city's second St. Nicholas's Church. The fine town houses surrounding the square are a study in different architectural styles, ranging from the genuine Gothic House at the Stone Bell to the 19th-century mock-Gothic No. 16.

WENCESLAS SQUARE

Despite its sometimes rather seedy air, Wenceslas Square (Václavské náměstí) is still the place where the city's heart beats most strongly, and to meet someone "beneath the horse" (the Wenceslas statue) remains a special thrill.

When is a square not a square? When it's a boulevard. "Václavák," 2,300 feet long, slopes gently up to the imposing façade of the National Museum (► 44), which is fronted by the statue of Wenceslas on his sprightly steed. This is a good place to arrange a rendezvous—whatever the time of day there's always some action, with daytime shoppers and sightseers replaced by every species of night owl as darkness falls.

Many of the dramas of modern times have been played out here. In 1918, the new state of Czechoslovakia was proclaimed here, and in 1939 German tanks underlined the republic's demise. In 1968, more tanks arrived—this time to crush the Prague Spring of Alexander Dubček. To protest the Soviet occupation, Jan Palach burned himself to death here the following year, and in 1989, Dubček and Václav Havel waved from the balcony of No. 36 as half a million Czechs crowded the square to celebrate the collapse of Communism.

Museum of modern architecture The procession of buildings lining both sides of the square, from the resplendent art-nouveau Hotel Evropa to the elegant Functionalist Bata Store, tells the story of the distinctively Czech contribution to 20th-century architecture and design. Even more intriguing are the arcades (*pasáž*) that burrow deep into the buildings, creating a labyrinthine world of boutiques, theaters, cafés, and cinemas.

HIGHLIGHTS

- St. Wenceslas statue, Josef Myslbek (1912)
- Arcades of the Lucerna Palace
- Grand Hotel Evropa, completed 1905 (No. 25)
- 1920s Functionalist Bata and Lindt buildings (Nos. 6, 12)
- Ambassador, late art-nouveau hotel of 1912 (No. 5)
- Memorial to the victims of Communism
- 1950s Soviet-style Jalta Hotel (No. 45)
- Former Bank of Moravia of 1916 (Nos. 38–40)
- Art-nouveau Peterka building of 1901 (No. 12)
- Koruna Palace of 1914 (No. 1)

INFORMATION

- 🗓 E4–F5
- ✉ Václavské náměstí, Nové město
- 🍴 Many restaurants and cafés
- Ⓜ Můstek or Muzeum
- ♿ Fair
- ↔ National Museum (► 44)

43

NATIONAL MUSEUM

HIGHLIGHTS

- Allegorical sculptures on the terrace
- The Pantheon and dome
- Coin collection
- Collection of precious stones
- Skeleton of a whale

INFORMATION

- ✚ F5
- ✉ Václavské náměstí 68, Nové město
- ☎ 2449 7111
- 🕐 Nov–Mar daily 9–5. Apr–Oct daily 10–6. Closed first Tue of month
- 🍴 Café
- Ⓜ Muzeum
- ♿ Few
- 💷 Moderate
- ↔ Wenceslas Square (▶ 43)

Some people find Prague's National Museum (Národní muzeum) disappointing, crammed as it is with cabinets full of beetles and mineral specimens. However, try to enjoy it as a period piece in its own right, for its dusty showcases are as venerable as the building itself.

Top building Its gilded dome crowning the rise at the top of Wenceslas Square, the prestigious National Museum provides a grand finale to the capital's most important street. The neo-Renaissance building was completed in 1891, and at the time was as much an object of pride to the Czech populace as the National Theater (▶ 36). Such is its presence that some visitors have mistaken it for the parliament building, as did the Soviet gunner who raked its façade with machine-gun fire in August 1968.

An array of -ologies Even if you are not an enthusiastic entomologist, paleontologist, zoologist, mineralogist, or numismatist, you can't fail to be impressed by the evidence assembled here of the 19th century's great passion for collecting and classifying. Perhaps more immediately attractive will be the temporary exhibitions, which draw on the museum's vast collections; the dinosaur display proves at least as compelling to young visitors as the famous film that may

Allegorical figure of the River Vltava, on the stairway leading up to the National Museum

have inspired it. Above all, the building itself is most impressive, with its grand stairways, statuary, mosaics, and patterned floors. And, unlike virtually every other attraction in Prague, it's open on Mondays.

22

NATIONAL TECHNICAL MUSEUM

Did you know that Czechoslovakia had one of the world's biggest auto industries and that Škoda cars are legendary for their toughness and reliability? That a horse-drawn railroad once linked Bohemia with Austria? That a Czechoslovak fleet once sailed the oceans?

Past glories The answer to all these questions will be "yes," after you've visited this wonderful museum (the Národní technické muzeum) off the beaten track on the edge of Letná Plain. The facelessness of the building belies the richness and fascination of its contents, a celebration of the longstanding technological prowess of inventive and hard-working Czechs. The Czech provinces were the industrial powerhouse of the Austro-Hungarian Empire, their steel works and coal mines providing the foundation for excellence in engineering of all kinds, from the production of weapons to locomotive manufacture. Later, between the two world wars, independent Czechoslovakia's light industries led the world in innovativeness and quality.

Trains and boats and planes The museum's collection of technological artifacts is displayed to spectacular effect in the vast glass-roofed and galleried main hall, where balloons and biplanes hang in space above ranks of sinister-looking streamlined limousines and powerful steam engines. The side galleries tell the story of "The Wheel" and of navigation, from rafting timber on the Vltava to transporting ore across the oceans in the Czechoslovak carrier *Košice*. Deep underground there's an exhibit of a coal mine, and other sections tell you all you ever wanted to know about time, sound, geodesy, photography, and astronomy.

HIGHLIGHTS

- 1928 Škoda fire engine
- Laurent and Klement soft-top roadster
- President Masaryk's V-12 Tatra
- Soviet ZIS 110B limousine
- Express locomotive 375-007 of 1911
- Imperial family's railway dining car of 1891
- Bleriot XI Kašpar monoplane
- Sokol monoplane

INFORMATION

✚ E3
✉ Kostelní 42/44, Holešovice
☎ 2039 9111
◷ Tue–Sun 9–5
🚋 Tram 26 to Letenské náměstí, or Metro Vltavská then Tram 1 to Letenské náměstí
♿ Few
▮ Moderate
↔ Museum of Modern Art (► 47), Letná Plain (► 50)

MUNICIPAL HOUSE

The prosaic name "Municipal House" fails utterly to convey anything of the character of the extraordinary art-nouveau Obecní dům, a gloriously extravagant turn-of-the-century confection on which every artist of the day seems to have left his stamp.

City council citadel Glittering like some gigantic, flamboyant jewel, more brightly than ever since its restoration in 1997, the Obecní dům is linked to the blackened Powder Tower (Prašná brána; ► 51), last relic of the Old Town's fortifications and for long one of the city's main symbols. The intention of the city fathers in the first years of the 20th century was to add an even more powerful element to the cityscape that would celebrate the glory of the Czech nation and Prague's place within it. The site of the old Royal Palace was selected, and no expense was spared to erect a megastructure in which the city's burgeoning life could expand.

Ornamental orgy The building program included meeting and assembly rooms, cafés, restaurants, bars, even a pâtisserie, and the mayor was provided with particularly luxurious quarters. The 1,149-seat Smetana Hall, later the home of the Czech Philharmonic, is a temple to the muse of Bohemian music. Everything, even the elevators, is encrusted with lavish decoration, including stucco, glass, mosaic, murals, textiles, and metalwork.

The glittering portal of the Municipal House

MUSEUM OF MODERN ART

"What I found to be a truly great experience was a tour of the Prague Trades Fair Building. The first impression created by the enormous palace is breathtaking." So enthused the great architect Le Corbusier when he visited Prague in 1928, shortly after this monumental structure, known in Czech as the Veletržní Palác, was completed.

Trailblazer Never lacking in ego, Le Corbusier was none the less vexed to find that his Czech colleagues had got in first in completing what is one of the key buildings in the evolution of 20th-century design, a secular, modern-day cathedral constructed in concrete, steel, and glass. Set in the suburb of Holešovice, the palace was intended to be a showpiece for the products of Czechoslovakia. However, trade fairs moved away from Prague to Brno, and for many years the great building languished in neglect and obscurity, its originality forgotten as its architectural innovations became the norm throughout the world.

Disguised blessing After fire gutted the palace in 1974, it was decided to use its elegant spaces to display the city's modern art treasures, which had previously been hidden away without a proper home. In all, it took nearly 20 years to complete restoration work, but the wait was well worthwhile. The core of the collection remains the amazing achievements of Czech painters and sculptors in the early part of the 20th century. It also shows works by the French Impressionists and other modern foreign paintings from the National Gallery, and promotes contemporary arts of all types, staging the kind of major international art shows of which the Czechs were so long deprived.

HIGHLIGHTS

- Reader of Dostoyevsky, Emil Filla
- Serie C VI, František Kupka
- Melancholy, Jan Zrzavý
- Sailor, Karel Dvořák
- Self-portrait, Picasso
- Self-portrait, Douanier Rousseau
- Green Rye, Van Gogh
- Virgin, Gustav Klimt
- Pregnant Woman and Death, Egon Schiele

INFORMATION

- ✚ F2
- ✉ Dukelských hrdinů 47, Holešovice
- ☎ 24 30 11 11
- 🕐 Tue–Wed, Fri–Sun 10–6; Thu 10–9
- 🍴 Restaurants and cafés
- 🚊 Tram 5 from Náměstí Republiky
- ♿ Few
- 💷 Moderate
- ↔ National Technical Museum (► 45)

Top: Green Rye, by Van Gogh

47

TROJA CHÂTEAU

HIGHLIGHTS

- Garden approach on river side of château
- South staircase and terrace with battling Titans
- Grand Hall paintings
- Šternberg Chapel
- Faïence collection

Nearby

- Prague Zoo
- Botanical Gardens
- St. Clair's Chapel

INFORMATION

- ✚ D1
- ✉ U trojského zámku 4, Troja
- ☎ 689 07 61
- 🕐 Apr–Oct Tue–Sun 10–6. Nov–Mar Sat–Sun 10–5
- 🍴 Restaurant
- Ⓜ Nádraží Holešovice, then Bus 112 to Zoologická zahrada
- 🚊 Tram 5 to Výstaviště, then walk across Stromovka Park and Imperial Island (Císařský ostrov) toward zoo
- ♿ Few
- 💷 Moderate
- ↔ Prague Zoo (▶ 59)

Out here you can catch a glimpse of how delightful Prague's countryside must have been three centuries ago, with vine-clad slopes, trees in abundance, plus the resplendent Baroque palace of Trojský zámek among the allées and parterres.

Prague's Versailles This extravagant palace was built not by the monarch, but by the second richest man in Prague, Count Wenceslas Adelbert Šternberg. The Šternbergs profited from the Thirty Years War, and at the end of the 17th century were in a position to commission Jean-Baptiste Mathey to design a country house along the lines of the contemporary châteaus of the architect's native France. The south-facing site by the river, oriented directly on St. Vitus's Cathedral and Prague Castle on the far side of the Royal Hunting Grounds (now Stromovka Park), was ideal for Šternberg, allowing him to offer the monarch the right kind of hospitality following a day's hunting.

Ornamental extravagance The palace's proportions are grandiose, and its painted interiors go over the top in paying homage to the country's Habsburg rulers. And over the top, too, goes a turbaned Turk as he topples, in stunning trompe-l'oeil, from the mock battlements in the grand hall. Troja was acquired by the state in the 1920s, but restored only in the late 1980s (some think excessively). It contains part of Prague's collection of 19th-century paintings, few of which can compete with the flamboyance of their setting.

Troja's grounds abound in ornamentation

PRAGUE's *best*

49

PANORAMAS

Across the river

Some of the finest views of Prague are those in which the city is seen across the broad waters of the Vltava, as from the Smetana statue or Kampa Island. A stroll along the embankments and footpaths on both sides of the river is equally rewarding, as are the islands—Slavonic Island (Slovanský ostrov) and Shooters' Island (Střelecký ostrov).

Malá Strana from Petřín

TOWER, ST. VITUS'S CATHEDRAL (KATEDRALA SVATÉHO VÍTA)

Climb the 287 steps of St. Vitus's Cathedral tower for one of the best all-round panoramas of the city and its surroundings, as well as close-ups of the exterior of the cathedral itself, with its bristling buttresses, diamond-tiled roofs, and copper cockerels atop spiky perches.

➕ C/D4 ✉ Pražský hrad 🕐 Apr–Oct daily 10–5 🍴 Cafés and restaurants 🚋 Tram 22 to Pražský hrad 🎫 Inexpensive

EMBANKMENT, KAMPA ISLAND

From the shady parkland of Kampa Island there is an unusual view across the Vltava over Charles Bridge and the foaming weir to the Old Town.

➕ D4 ✉ U Sovových mlýnů 🕐 Permanently open 🚋 Trams 12, 22 to Hellichova 🎫 Free

LETNÁ PLAIN (LETENSKÉ SADY)

The parks and gardens of Letná Plain stretch from the eastern end of Prague Castle high above the north bank of the Vltava. Between 1955 and 1962 a monster statue of Stalin stood here. The plinth, now infested with skateboarders, is occupied by a giant metronome, and makes an excellent vantage point over the river, its bridges, and the Old Town.

➕ D–E3 ✉ Letenské sady 🕐 Permanently accessible 🚇 Malostranská and uphill walk 🚋 Tram 18 to Chotkovy sady or 22 to Kralovský letohrádek 🎫 Free

OLD ROYAL PALACE (STARÝ KRÁLOVSKÝ PALÁC)

After admiring the interiors of the Old Royal Palace and the Vladislav Hall, take a stroll on the south-facing terrace or peep through the windows from which the Catholic councellors were thrown out in 1618 (▶ 12). All Prague lies at your feet.

➕ D4 ✉ Pražský hrad ☎ 2437 3368 🕐 Apr–Oct Tue–Sun 9–5. Nov–Mar Tue–Sun 9–4 🍴 Cafés and restaurants 🚋 Tram 22 to Pražský hrad 🎫 Moderate

TOWER, OLD TOWN HALL (STAROMĚSTSKÁ RADNICE)

The climb up the tower of the Old Town Hall is well worthwhile for the dizzying view it gives of the swarming activity in Old Town Square, as well as of the hig-gledy-piggledy red-tiled roofs of the medieval Old Town.

➕ E4 ✉ Staroměstské náměstí ☎ 2448 3254 🕐 Apr–Sep Mon 11–6; Tue–Sun 9–6. Oct–Mar Mon 11–5; Tue–Sun 9–5 🍴 Restaurants in square 🚇 Staroměstská 🎫 Moderate

PETŘÍN HILL LOOKOUT TOWER (ROZHLEDNA)
This little brother of the Eiffel Tower was erected for Prague's great Jubilee Expo of 1891. Prepare to climb 299 steps!
➕ C4 ✉ Petřín ⏱ Apr–Aug daily 10–7. Sep–Oct daily 10–6. Nov–Mar Sat–Sun 10–5 🚋 Tram 12 or 22 to Hellichova, then Lanovka funicular (from Újezd) 💰 Moderate

POWDER TOWER (PRAŠNÁ BRÁNA)
The sumptuous roofscape of the adjoining Municipal House (Obecní dům; ➤ 46) makes an immediate impact, but this panorama is particularly appealing because of the vista along Celetná Street into the heart of the Old Town.
➕ E/F4 ✉ Náměstí Republiky ⏱ Winter daily 10–5. Summer daily 10–6 🚇 Náměstí Republiky 🚋 Trams 5, 14 to Náměstí Republiky 💰 Moderate

SMETANA STATUE
The walkway leading to the Smetana Museum (➤ 57) is in fact a pier (known as Novotného lávka), built out into the river. At its very tip are café tables and a statue of the composer; the view across the river, whose roaring weir drowns all intrusive noises, is the classic one of Charles Bridge, Malá Strana, and Prague Castle above.
➕ D4 ✉ Novotného lávka ⏱ Permanently open 🍴 Café and restaurant 🚇 Staroměstská 🚋 Trams 17, 18 to Karlovy lázně 💰 Free

TELEVISION TOWER (TELEVIZNÍ VYSÍLAČ)
This immense television transmitter tower in the inner suburb of Žižkov, 709 feet tall, may be a blot on Prague's townscape (see panel), but its gallery does give visitors stupendous views over the city and its surroundings. The best time to take the elevator to the top is fairly early in the day, before the sun has moved too far round to the west.
➕ G5 ✉ Mahlerovy sady ☎ 6700 5784 🍴 Restaurant 🚇 Jiřího z Poděbrad 🚋 Trams 5, 9, 26 to Lipanská 💰 Moderate

VYŠEHRAD
A walk around the ramparts of the old fortifications of Vyšehrad gives contrasting views along the Vltava flowing far below. Upstream, Prague is surprisingly countrified, with rugged limestone crags and rough woodland, while downstream the panorama reveals the city, especially Hradčany, from an entirely new angle. Nearby, the terraces of the Communists' huge Palace of Culture offer a view across the deep Nusle ravine toward the New Town, guarded by the walls and cupolas of the Karlov Monastery.
➕ E6/7 ✉ Vyšehrad ⏱ Permanently accessible 🍴 Café and restaurant 🚇 Vyšehrad 🚋 Trams 3, 7, 17 to Výtoň

Old Town Square from the Old Town Hall tower

Unpopular neighbor
Building the unlovely TV tower in Žižkov necessitated destroying part of an old Jewish cemetery and was resisted by locals and other protesters (insofar as any resistance was possible in Communist days). Some people are still uneasy, claiming that they pick up transmissions on virtually any metal object, or that their bodies are being slowly microwaved.

GALLERIES

Unseen art

Housing Prague's vast and varied art collections has always posed problems. Under Communism, many pictures and other art objects were kept more or less permanently in storage, and the unique Czech contribution to 20th-century art has never been properly celebrated. The big issue is now a financial one. If there are particular works you want to see, it's worth checking first whether they are actually on display.

GOLTZ-KINSKÝ PALACE
(PALÁC GOLTZ-KINSKÝCH)

Changing exhibitions, based on the National Gallery's vast collections of prints and drawings. It was from a balcony here that Klement Gottwald proclaimed the victory of the working classes in 1948.
✚ E4 ✉ Staroměstské náměstí 12 ☎ 24 81 07 58 ⏰ Reopening in 1999 after reconstruction 🍴 Cafés and restaurants in Old Town Square 🚇 Staroměstská 💵 Moderate

HOUSE AT THE STONE BELL
(DŮM U KAMENNÉHO ZVONU)

For many years this fine town house, now displaying art by young Czech contemporaries, was thought to be a rococo palace. When the restorers began work on it, that rarity, a Gothic mansion, was discovered behind the 18th-century work. After much debate, the building was restored to its medieval state.
✚ E4 ✉ Staroměstské náměstí 13 ☎ 2482 7526 ⏰ Tue–Sun 10–6 🍴 Cafés and restaurants in Old Town Square 🚇 Staroměstská 💵 Moderate

House at the Stone Bell

LAPIDÁRIUM

Classical and modern sculpture, including some of the original statues from Charles Bridge brought here to protect them.
✚ F2 ✉ Výstaviště, Holešovice ☎ 2422 6488 ⏰ Fri 12–6; Sat–Sun 10–12:30, 1–6 🍴 Restaurants and cafés in grounds 🚇 Nádraží Holešovice 🚊 Trams 5, 12, 17 to Výstaviště 💵 Inexpensive

RIDING SCHOOL OF PRAGUE
CASTLE (JÍZDÁRNA)

This big Baroque building is used by the National Gallery for temporary exhibitions.
✚ C3 ✉ U Prašného mostu 55, Hradčany ☎ 2437 3368 ⏰ Tue–Sun 10–6 🍴 Cafés and restaurants in castle 🚊 Tram 22 to Pražský hrad 💵 Moderate

MUSEUMS

See Top 25 Sights for
DECORATIVE ARTS MUSEUM ➤ 37
NATIONAL MUSEUM ➤ 44
NATIONAL TECHNICAL MUSEUM ➤ 45
STATE JEWISH MUSEUM ➤ 40

CITY MUSEUM
(MUZEUM HLAVNÍHO MĚSTA PRAHY)
This pompous late 19th-century building contains exhibits telling the story of Prague's evolution from the earliest times. The star is an extraordinary scale model of the city as it was in the 1820s and 1830s, meticulously put together by a person of infinite patience named Antonín Langweil. Most of the extensive collections are in storage, but selections (posters, postcards, etc.) are shown in rotation.
✚ F4 ✉ Na poříčí 52, north Nové město ☎ 2481 6772
🕐 Tue–Sun 10–6 🚇 Florenc 🎟 Inexpensive

MILITARY MUSEUM, SCHWARZENBERG PALACE
(VOJENSKÉ MUZEUM)
Behind the stunning sgraffito façades of this Renaissance palace is an array of militaria of all kinds —guns, uniforms, models, paintings, maps—proving what a bloody battleground this part of Central Europe always was.
✚ C4 ✉ Hradčanské náměstí 2, Hradčany ☎ 2020 2020
🕐 May–Oct Tue–Sun 10–6 🚇 Malostranská 🚊 Tram 22 to Pražský hrad 🎟 Inexpensive

NÁPRSTEK MUSEUM (NÁPRSTKOVO MUZEUM)
Intriguing ethnographical exhibits assembled by a 19th-century collector in love with the indigenous cultures of the Americas and Pacific.
✚ E4 ✉ Betlémské náměstí 1, Staré město ☎ 24 21 45 37
🕐 Tue–Sun 9–12, 12:45–5:30 🚇 Staroměstská or Národní třída 🎟 Inexpensive

POLICE MUSEUM (MUZEUM POLICIE ČR)
This museum recovered quickly from the collapse of the old order in 1989 and gives an upbeat account of Czech policing, with plenty of gore and weaponry on show in, incongruously, what was once the Karlov Monastery.
✚ E6 ✉ Ke Karlovu 1, Nové město ☎ 29 52 09 🕐 Tue–Sun 10–5 🚇 I. P. Pavlova or Vyšehrad 🎟 Inexpensive

POSTAL MUSEUM (POŠTOVNÍ MUZEUM)
A delightful little museum of great appeal, and not just to philatelists. It's housed in an attractive building with some charming 19th-century frescoes.
✚ F3 ✉ Nové mlýny 2, north Nové město ☎ 23 12 060
🕐 Tue–Sun 9–5 🚇 Náměstí Republiky, then Tram 5, 14 to Dlouhá třída 🎟 Inexpensive

The big guns
Czech and Slovak involvement in the big conflict that never happened, the face-off of the Cold War, is chillingly displayed in the huge collection of military hardware on show at the Aircraft Museum (Letecké muzeum) at Kbely airfield on the city's eastern outskirts. Some of the aircraft date back to World War I, but above all it's the Russian MiG jetfighters that remain in the memory.

More militaria
Almost unknown abroad, the tale of Czech and Slovak involvement in the conflicts of the 20th century is told in the Museum of the Resistance and History of the Army (Muzeum odboje a dějin armady), at the foot of the National Memorial in the inner suburb of Žižkov.

PALACES

Auto sculpture

In summer 1989, the streets around the West German Embassy were clogged with Wartburgs and Trabants abandoned by their East German owners. A fiberglass Trabant on mighty legs now stands in the embassy garden as a memorial to those days.

Coat of arms, Archbishop's Palace

High diplomacy

The Anglophile and athletic first president of Czechoslovakia, Tomáš Masaryk, is said to have maintained good relations with the British ambassador in the Thun Palace by climbing down a ladder set against Prague Castle's walls to drop in for tea.

> **See Top 25 Sights for**
> **ROYAL PALACE ➤ 29**
> **ŠTERNBERG PALACE ➤ 27**
> **WALLENSTEIN PALACE ➤ 34**

ARCHBISHOP'S PALACE (ARCIBISKUPSKÝ PALÁC)

The lusciously restored rococo façade hides a sumptuous residence, unfortunately accessible only on special occasions.
🕂 C4 ✉ Hradčanské náměstí 16 🕐 Not normally open to the public 🚋 Tram 22 to Pražský hrad

ČERNÍN PALACE (ČERNÍNSKÝ PALÁC)

It was from this huge Baroque structure (completed 1720), now the Foreign Ministry, that Jan Masaryk fell to his death in 1948.
🕂 C4 ✉ Loretánské náměstí, Hradčany 🕐 Not open to the public 🚋 Tram 22 to Pohořelec

HOUSE OF THE LORDS OF KUNŠTÁT AND PODĚBRADY (DŮM PÁNŮ Z KUNŠTÁTU A PODĚBRAD)

Possibly the most ancient interior accessible to the public is this 13th-century mansion of King George of Poděbrady.
🕂 E4 ✉ Řetězová 3, Staré město 🕐 Summer daily 10–6. Closed winter 🚇 Staroměstská 🎟 Inexpensive

LOBKOVIC PALACE (LOBKOVICKÝ PALÁC)

This superb Baroque structure (not to be confused with the Lobkovic Palace within the castle precinct), the residence of the German ambassador, saw strange scenes in summer 1989, when it became a temporary home to thousands of East Germans seeking refuge.
🕂 C4 ✉ Vlašská 19 🕐 Not open to the public 🚋 Tram 12, 22 to Malostranské náměstí

SCHÖNBORN-COLLOREDO PALACE (SCHÖNBORNSKÝ PALÁC)

The U.S. Embassy occupies a Baroque palace whose grandeur equals that of the nearby German Embassy.
🕂 D4 ✉ Tržiště 15, Malá Strana 🕐 Not open to the public 🚋 Tram 12, 22 to Malostranské náměstí

SCHWARZENBERG PALACE ➤ 53

THUN PALACE (THUNOVSKÝ PALÁC)

The British Embassy since 1918. Presented by the emperor in 1630 to Walter Leslie, a Scotsman who had helped assassinate Wallenstein, the emperor's great rival.
🕂 D4 ✉ Thunovská 25, Malá Strana 🕐 Not open to the public 🚇 Malostranská

CHURCHES

See Top 25 Sights for
LORETTO SHRINE ➤ 26
ST. GEORGE'S BASILICA ➤ 31
ST. NICHOLAS'S CHURCH, MALÁ STRANA ➤ 33
ST. VITUS'S CATHEDRAL ➤ 30

BETHLEHEM CHAPEL (BETLÉMSKÁ KAPLE)
You must see this barn-like structure where Jan Hus preached to really appreciate the deeply nonconformist traditions so thoroughly obscured by centuries of imposed Catholicism. The Baroque architecture is extravagant.
➕ E4 ✉ Betlémské náměstí, Staré město ⏰ Apr–Oct daily 9–6. Nov–Mar daily 9–5 🍴 Restaurants and cafés nearby 🚇 Národní třída 🎟 Inexpensive

CHURCH OF OUR LADY VICTORIOUS (KOSTEL PANNY MARIE VÍTĚZNÉ)
After Czech Protestantism was crushed in 1621, this church became a center of the Counter-Reformation, thanks not least to miracles wrought by the Bambino di Praga waxwork (see panel).
➕ D4 ✉ Karmelitská 9, Malá Strana ⏰ Daily 7–9 🚋 Tram 12, 22 to Malostranské náměstí

ST. JAMES'S CHURCH (KOSTEL SVATÉHO JAKUBA)
Beneath the Baroque froth is an ancient Gothic church, though you'd hardly guess it. The acoustics of the long nave are particularly impressive, and concerts held here are generally well attended.
➕ E4 ✉ Malá Štupartská, Staré město ⏰ Daily 9:30–4 🚇 Náměstí Republiky

ST. NICHOLAS'S CHURCH, OLD TOWN (KOSTEL SVATÉHO MIKULÁŠE, STARÉ MĚSTO)
St. Nicholas's twin towers and grand dome are the work of the great Baroque architect, Kilian Ignaz Dientzenhofer. His church is now a prominent feature of Old Town Square, but it was originally designed to fit into the narrow street that once ran here.
➕ E4 ✉ Staroměstské náměstí, Staré město ⏰ Tue, Thu–Fri 10–12; Wed 10–12, 2–4; Sun 9:30–10:30, 11:30–12 🚇 Staroměstská

TÝN CHURCH (KOSTEL PANNY MARIE PŘED TÝNEM)
Among the city's best-known landmarks is the Gothic Týn Church, whose twin towers stick up spikily behind the houses east of Old Town Square. Inside are some fascinating tombs.
➕ E4 ✉ Týnská and Celetná, Staré město ⏰ May only be open for services due to reconstruction 🍴 Cafés and restaurants nearby 🚇 Staroměstská or Náměstí Republiky

Týn Church

Rough justice
A withered hand hangs from the altar in St. James's Church, severed by a butcher when the thief to whom it belonged was apprehended by the Virgin Mary, who refused to let go.

Bambino di Praga
The Bambino di Praga waxwork was given to the Church of Our Lady Victorious in 1628 as part of the re-Catholicization imposed on the wayward Czechs. The miracles performed by the diminutive effigy of the infant Jesus are even more numerous than its 60 sumptuous changes of outfit.

TWENTIETH-CENTURY BUILDINGS

See Top 25 Sights for
MUNICIPAL HOUSE (OBECNÍ DŮM) ➤ 46
**VELETRŽNÍ PALÁC, MUSEUM OF
MODERN ART** ➤ 47

Art nouveau

The glorious effusions of art nouveau, with its use of sinuous lines and motifs from the natural world, mark the townscape all over the city. Prague rivals Vienna in the number of edifices built in this style, known here as Secession.

The famous Black Madonna

Czech innovations

Art nouveau/Secession was an international style, but later Czech architects created unique movements of their own—Rondo-Cubism, for instance, and the more sober, Functionalist style that then followed.

BANK OF THE LEGIONS (BANKA LEGIÍ)

Czechoslovak legionaries fought on many fronts in World War I, and the sculptures decorating the façade of this handsome Rondo-Cubist (see panel) building of 1923 commemorate their exploits.
➕ F4 ✉ Na poříčí 24, north Nové město 🕓 Accessible during banking hours to customers of Komerční Banka 🚇 Náměstí Republiky

CUBIST STREETLAMP

This extraordinary little object, an echo of Czech Cubism, still seems to vibrate with the artistic excitements that suffused metropolitan life in early 20th-century Prague.
➕ E5 ✉ Jungmannovo náměstí, Nové město 🚇 Můstek

HOUSE AT THE BLACK MADONNA (DŮM U ČERNÉ MATKY BOŽÍ)

This striking example of Czech Cubist architecture, designed by Josef Gočár (1912), stands challengingly at the corner of Celetná Street in the heart of the Old Town, yet somehow manages to harmonize with its surroundings. Look for the Black Madonna in her gilded cage.
➕ E4 ✉ Ovocný trh 19, Staré město 🕓 Art gallery: Tue–Sun 10–6 🍴 Restaurant 🚇 Náměstí Republiky 💰 Inexpensive

MAIN STATION (HLAVNÍ NÁDRAŽÍ)

Above the modern concourses rise the richly ornamented art-nouveau buildings of Prague's main station (1909), originally named after Emperor Franz Josef, then after President Wilson.
➕ F4 ✉ Wilsonova 8, Nové město 🕓 24 hours 🍴 Buffet 🚇 Hlavní nádraží 💰 Free

NOS. 7 & 9 NÁRODNÍ TŘÍDA

Fascinating variations on the theme of art nouveau can be traced in the façades of these adjoining office buildings. Both were designed by Osvald Polívka; No. 9 was built for the publisher Topič, and No. 7 for an insurance company.
➕ E5 ✉ Národní třída 7 & 9, Nové město 🚇 Národní třída

U NOVÁKŮ

This lavishly decorated art-nouveau structure, now a casino, was built as a department store in 1903. The colorful mosaic, by Jan Preisler, flowing over its façade, represents Trade and Industry.
➕ E5 ✉ Vodičkova 30, Nové město 🕓 Open to customers of Varieté Praga 🍴 Restaurant 🚇 Můstek

FOR MUSIC LOVERS

See Top 25 Sights for
NATIONAL THEATER
(NÁRODNÍ DIVADLO) ➤ 36
ST. NICHOLAS'S CHURCH, MALÁ STRANA ➤ 33

DVOŘÁK'S BIRTHPLACE

Dvořák was born the son of an innkeeper in the unassuming little village of Nelahozeves on the Elbe River. His birthplace, at the foot of the Lobkovic family's huge Renaissance castle, is now a museum.
🚌 Off map, about 20 miles northwest of Prague ✉ Nelahozeves 12 🕐 Tue–Sun 9–12, 2–5 🚉 Nelahozeves 💷 Inexpensive

DVOŘÁK MUSEUM (VILA AMERIKA)

This exquisite little villa was built for Count Michna in 1720 as a summer retreat, when this part of the New Town was still countryside. It now serves as a fascinating repository for Dvořák memorabilia (➤ 76).
🚌 E6 ✉ Ke Karlovu 20, Nové město ☎ 29 82 14 🕐 Tue–Sun 10–5 🚋 I. P. Pavlova 💷 Inexpensive

ESTATES THEATER (STAVOVSKÉ DIVADLO) ➤ 75

MOZART MUSEUM (BERTRAMKA)

Mozart's closest friends in Prague were the Dušeks, and the Bertramka was their rural retreat. This is the place where the great composer dashed off the last lines of *Don Giovanni* before conducting its premiere in the Estates Theater (➤ 75).
🚌 C6 ✉ Mozartova 169, Smíchov ☎ 54 38 93 🕐 Apr–Oct daily 9:30–6. Nov–Mar daily 9:30–5 🚇 Anděl, then Tram 4, 7, 9 to Bertramka (one stop) 💷 Inexpensive

SMETANA HALL (SMETANOVA SÍŇ)

The highly decorated Smetana Hall is the grandest space in the Municipal House (➤ 46), with seating for 1,149. The Prague Spring music festival is heralded here every year with a rousing rendition of the symphonic poem *Má vlast* (*My Country*).
🚌 E/F4 ✉ Obecní dům, Náměstí Republiky ☎ 2200 2100 🕐 Check locally for times of guided tours 🍴 Café and restaurant 🚇 Náměstí Republiky

SMETANA MUSEUM
(MUSEUM BEDŘICHA SMETANY)

The museum dedicated to the composer of "Vltava" is appropriately sited in a building that rises directly out of the river.
🚌 D4 ✉ Novotného lávka 1, Staré město ☎ 2422 9075 🕐 Wed–Mon 10–5 🚇 Staroměstská

STATE OPERA (STÁTNÍ OPERA PRAHA – SMETANA DIVADLO) ➤ 75

A musical nation

Co Čech—to muzikant! ("All Czechs are musicians!") goes the saying, and this is certainly one of the most musical of nations. In the 18th century Bohemia supplied musicians and composers to the whole of Europe.

Music for free

By all means go to concerts at the places listed on this page. But bearing in mind that "all Czechs are musicians," you should also try to enjoy the often very high-quality music made by street performers. If you keep your ears cocked, you may even catch one of tomorrow's virtuosi practicing at an open window.

Dvořák's piano, Vila Amerika

GREEN SPACES

Monkish retreat

The old garden of the Franciscan monks between Wenceslas Square (Václavské náměstí) and Jungmann Square (Jungmannovo náměstí) is a welcome oasis in the heart of the city.

See Top 25 Sights for
PETŘÍN HILL ➤ 28
WALLENSTEIN GARDENS ➤ 34

BAROQUE GARDENS BELOW THE CASTLE
The aristocrats in their palaces in Malá Strana at the foot of Prague Castle turned their interconnecting gardens into a paradise of arbors, gazebos, fountains, and stairways. Now partially reopened after restoration, they can also be enjoyed from the castle's Ramparts Garden above.
D4 Pražský hrad, Hradčany Daily Malostranská Inexpensive

KAMPA ISLAND
Kampa Island was flooded regularly until the Vltava was tamed in the 1950s, discouraging building and leaving large parts of it undeveloped.
D4–5 At all times Tram 12, 22 to Hellichova or Malostranské náměstí Free

LETNÁ PLAIN (LETENSKÉ SADY) ➤ 50

Stromovka Park, Holešovice

RAMPARTS GARDEN (ZAHRADA NA VALECH)
The gardens just to the south of the castle were redesigned in the 1920s and embellished with carefully placed sculptural objects, including a miniature pyramid.
C–D4 Pražský hrad, Hradčany Summer 10–6. Closed winter Malostranská then uphill walk Tram 22 to Pražský hrad Free

ROYAL GARDENS (KRÁLOVSKÁ ZAHRADA)
Fine old trees and formal gardens make a superb setting for several pleasure pavilions north of the castle: the Baroque Riding School (➤ 52), the sgraffitoed Ball-Game Hall, and the beautiful Belvedere.
C/D3 Královský letohrádek, Hradčany Summer 10–6. Closed winter Tram 22 to Královský letohrádek Free

VOJAN GARDENS (VOJANOVY SADY)
A quiet retreat hidden away behind Malá Strana.
D4 U lužického semináře Daily 8–7 Malostranská Free

VRTBA GARDEN (VRTBOVSKÁ ZAHRADA)
Prague's finest individual Baroque garden has a splendid staircase, sculptures, and a view over Malá Strana.
D4 Karmelitská 18, Malá Strana May–Jun, Sep–Oct daily 10–4. Jul–Aug daily 10–6 Tram 12, 22 to Malostranské náměstí

Charles Square

Charles Square (Karlovo náměstí) is more of a park than a square, and is a useful resting place when pounding the sidewalks becomes too tiring in this spread-out part of town.

ATTRACTIONS FOR CHILDREN

See Top 25 Sights for
NATIONAL TECHNICAL MUSEUM ➤ 45
PETŘÍN HILL, WITH FUNICULAR,
   VIEWING TOWER, HALL OF MIRRORS,
   OBSERVATORY ➤ 28

ASTRONOMICAL CLOCK (ORLOJ)

Crowds gather every hour on the hour in front of the
Old Town Hall to enjoy the performance put on by
this fascinating clock, which not only tells the time
but gives the position of the sun, moon, and much
more, while the splendid painted calendar shows
saints' days, the signs of the zodiac, and the labors of
the months. Legend has it that Hanuš, the master
technician who perfected the mechanism, was
blinded by the city fathers to stop him passing his
secrets on. But Hanuš persuaded an apprentice to
lead him up inside the clock. He then plunged his
hands into the mechanism, putting it out of action
for 80 years.

➕ E4 ✉ Staroměstské náměstí ⏱ Performances daily on the hour
9–9 🚇 Staroměstská 🎫 Free

CHANGING OF THE GUARD

The blue-uniformed Castle Guard is ceremonially
relieved every day at noon, with extra buglers and
pomp on Sundays.

➕ C4 ✉ Pražský hrad, Hradčany ⏱ Daily at noon 🚋 Tram 22 to
Pražský hrad 🎫 Free

EXHIBITION GROUNDS (VÝSTAVIŠTĚ)

The extensive Exhibition Grounds in the inner
suburb of Holešovice have old-fashioned rides
among other attractions.

➕ E–F2 ✉ U Výstaviště, Holešovice ☎ 2010 3204 ⏱ Tue–Fri
from 2PM; Sat–Sun from 10AM (evening opening for performances)
🍴 Cafés and restaurants 🚋 Tram 5, 12, 17 to Výstaviště
🎫 Inexpensive

HISTORIC TRAM RIDE

A vintage tram trundles round a circuit linking the
city center, Malá Strana, and the Exhibition Grounds.

MILITARY MUSEUM (VOJENSKÉ MUZEUM) ➤ 53

PUPPET THEATERS ➤ 80

ZOO (ZOOLOGICKÁ ZAHRADA)

Not world-class, but useful to know about and
conveniently placed opposite Troja Château (➤ 48).

➕ D1 ✉ U Trojského zámku 3, Troja ☎ 688 04 80 ⏱ Mar–Apr
daily 9–5. May daily 9–6. Jun–Sep daily 9–7. Oct–Feb daily 9–4
🍴 Buffet 🚇 Nádraží Holešovice, then Bus 112 to Zoologická zahrada
🎫 Inexpensive

Keeping 'em happy

There are enough jazz bands,
sword-swallowers, and
other entertainers on the streets
to keep kids happily staring for
hours, not to mention any
number of tall towers to climb.
Incorrigible junior consumers will
find their favorite soft drinks, the
local ice cream is excellent, and
Prague is no longer a "One-Mac-
city;" the famous hamburgers are
for sale at several locations; and
pizzas and similar snacks are
available as well.

Getting around

Tram rides are a novelty to
many children—and excellent
for getting to know the city.
Other entertaining ways of
moving around include the
"train" that chugs up to Prague
Castle from Old Town Square
and the horse-drawn carriages,
also based in Old Town Square.

COMMUNIST MEMENTOES

Communist corruption

Despite being lowered every evening into a refrigerated chamber and receiving the attentions of the best embalmers available, the corpse of Klement Gottwald (1896–1954, Czechoslovakia's first Communist president), in the National Memorial, continued to putrefy. When platoons of Young Pioneers were brought to admire their leader, most of what they saw was not Klement, but skillfully crafted replacement parts.

Home sweet home

Paneláks (see main text) are regarded with a mixture of affection and exasperation. Any accommodations are desirable in a city with an acute housing shortage, especially if they are supplied with hot and cold running water and central heating like most *paneláks*. The downside is the dreariness of the surroundings.

BAROLOMĚJSKÁ POLICE STATION

The police station where Václav Havel was regularly brought in for interrogation in his dissident days has now been returned to its former owners, an order of nuns, who have leased part of it as a pension. If you book far enough ahead, you can spend the night in Havel's cell.

🞣 E4/5 ✉ Cloister Inn, Bartolomějská 9, Staré město
☎ 232 12 89 🚇 Národní třída 🛈 Accessible only to pension guests

HOLIDAY INN PRAGUE

A totally authentic example of the monumental wedding-cake architecture of the Stalinist era.

🞣 C2 ✉ Koulova 15, Dejvice ☎ 24 39 31 11 🍴 Café and restaurant 🚇 Dejvická 🚃 Tram 20, 25 to Podbaba 🛈 Expensive to stay

JAN PALACH'S GRAVE

The grave of the self-immolating student Jan Palach (➤ 43) is in the vast cemetery at Olšany. A square in the Old Town is also named after him, and flowers are regularly placed on the spot in Wenceslas Square where he died.

🞣 H–J5 ✉ Olšanské hřbitovy (Olšany cemetery), Vinohradská 🕐 Daily 8–7 🚇 Flóra or Želivského 🛈 Free

MEMORIAL TO NOVEMBER 17, 1989

In an arcade on Národní třída, a little memorial panel of hands raised in supplication marks where 50,000 student demonstrators were attacked by riot police—an event seen as the genesis of the Velvet Revolution.

🞣 E5 ✉ Národní třída 16, Nové město 🚇 Národní třída 🛈 Free

THE METRO

Prague's immaculate Metro once sported a number of fine examples of Socialist-Realist art. The only one remaining is the mosaic of a chisel-chinned worker and his mate at Anděl station.

🞣 D6 🕐 5ᴀᴍ–midnight 🚇 Anděl

NATIONAL MEMORIAL (NÁRODNÍ PAMÁTNÍK)

Built in the interwar period, this slab of a building atop the steep rise to the east of the downtown area served as a shrine to prominent Communist Party men. The memorial's future is uncertain.

🞣 G4 ✉ U památníku, Žižkov, Prague 3 🚇 Florenc then uphill walk 🚃 133, 207

PANELÁKS

All around the outskirts of Prague are the monolithic housing estates composed of high-rise blocks nicknamed *paneláks*, system-built on the Soviet model from concrete panels manufactured on site.

PRAGUE
where to...

CZECH CUISINE

Prices
Expect to pay for dinner per person without drinks:
$$$ over Kč600
$$ Kč200–600
$ Kč100–200

Dumplings

Love them or leave them, *knedliky* (dumplings) are the inevitable accompaniment to much Czech cooking, adding further solidity to an already substantial cuisine. Every housewife has her prized recipe, using bread, flour, potatoes, or semolina, and the homemade *knedlik* may have a lightness often absent from a restaurant's offering.

DERBY ($)
Basic soup and sandwich lunch for just a few crowns.
🔢 F2 ✉ Dukelských hrdinů 20
🚊 Tram 5, 12, 17 to Veletržní

FREGATA ($$)
An alternative to the Vltava (➤ 63) for traditional fish dishes.
🔢 E6 ✉ Ladova 3
☎ 29 31 21 🚇 Karlovo náměstí

MALOSTRANSKÁ BESEDA ($)
Czech food in Malá Strana Square.
🔢 D4 ✉ Malostranské náměstí ☎ 53 55 28
🚇 Malostranská

MYSLIVNA ($$)
Improbably located in a back street in suburban Vinohrady, "The Hunter's Lodge" is worth seeking out for its delicious game dishes.
🔢 G5 ✉ Jagellonská 21, Vinohrady ☎ 627 02 09
🚇 Jiřího z Poděbrad

NA OŘECHOVCE ($$)
Pub-restaurant with some of the city's best Czech food, deep in the garden suburb of Ořechovka ("Walnut Grove").
🔢 B3 ✉ Východní 7, Dejvice ☎ 312 48 42
🚊 Tram 1, 2, 18 to Sibeliova

NA RYBÁRNĚ ($$)
Fishy delights in a restaurant supposedly once frequented by President Havel and cronies.
🔢 E5/6 ✉ Gorazdova 17, Nové město ☎ 29 97 95
🚇 Karlovo náměstí

PLZEŇSKÁ RESTAURACE ($$)
In the basement of the beautifully restored Municipal House (➤ 46) is this art-nouveau designer's idea of what a Bohemian beer hall should look like.
🔢 E/F4 ✉ Náměstí Republiky 5, Staré město ☎ 2200 2763
🚇 Náměstí Republiky

POD KŘÍDLEM ($$$)
Stylish surroundings and impeccable food. Also conveniently close to the National Theater.
🔢 E5 ✉ Národní třída 10, Nové město ☎ 24 91 23 77
🚇 Národní třída

RESTAURACE NA POŘÍČÍ ($)
An unpretentious but well-run corner restaurant frequented mostly by locals but happy to welcome tourists. Close to Masaryk station and the Municipal House.
🔢 F4 ✉ Na poříčí 20, Nové město ☎ 2481 1363
🚇 Náměstí Republiky

RESTAURANT KRÁLE JIŘÍHO ($)
A useful port of call in suburban Vinohrady.
🔢 G5 ✉ Slavíkova 6 ☎ 627 29 69 🚇 Jiřího z Poděbrad

STARÁ RADNICE ($$)
A handy lunch-stop along the Hradčany tourist trail.
🔢 C4 ✉ Loretánská 1, Hradčany ☎ 2051 1140.
🚊 Tram 22 to Pražský hrad or Pohořelec

U BENEDIKTA ($$)
Conventional Czech cooking with some sophistication, served

in a patio behind the big Kotva department store.

➕ E4 ✉ Benediktská 11, Staré město ☎ 2481 3872 Ⓜ Náměstí Republiky

U ČIŽKŮ ($$)

Attractive Old Bohemian farmhouse setting with meaty specialties to match, such as platters of duck, pork, and sausage with dumplings and sauerkraut.

➕ E5 ✉ Karlovo náměstí 34, Nové město ☎ 29 88 91 Ⓜ Karlovo náměstí

U KALICHA ($$$)

Thanks to the Good Soldier Švejk's patronage in Austro-Hungarian days, this place is popular with visitors from abroad familiar with the famous Czech antihero. Solid food among much Švejkian memorabilia.

➕ E/F5/6 ✉ Na bojišti 12–14, Nové město ☎ 29 07 01 or 29 19 45 Ⓜ I. P. Pavlova

U MATOUŠE ($)

Traditional dishes plus innovative but still authentic explorations into what Czech (and Moravian) cuisine is all about. Give 24 hours notice if you want to feast on roast duckling cooked as it really should be.

➕ D5 ✉ Preslova 17, Smíchov ☎ 54 62 84 or 54 18 77 Ⓜ Anděl

U MĚSTSKÉ KNIHOVNY ($)

Solid local food in a totally unpretentious atmosphere.

➕ E4 ✉ Valentinská 11, Staré město ☎ 232 17 16 or 231 08 67 Ⓜ Staroměstská

U MIKULÁŠE DAČICKÉHO ($$)

Set designers from the famous Barrandov film studios fitted out this Czech restaurant as a medieval banqueting hall in the 1920s. Hearty food.

➕ D5 ✉ Viktora Huga 2, Smíchov ☎ 54 93 12 Ⓜ Closed Sun Ⓜ Anděl

U PASTÝŘKY ($$)

The rustic log cabin with a big open fireplace at "The Little Shepherdess" is an alternative to the Pezinok (▶ 62).

➕ F5/6 ✉ Bělehradská 15, Nusle ☎ 691 35 55 Ⓜ I. P. Pavlova 🚊 Tram 11

U PLEBÁNA ($$)

Any old prole can eat here now, though before 1989 "The Plebeian" was the preserve of Communist Party bigwigs. Now local and foreign business folk enjoy juicy duckling and succulent mixed grills.

➕ E4 ✉ Betlémské náměstí 10, Staré město ☎ 24 22 90 23 Ⓜ Národní třída

VLTAVA ($)

Soup, carp, and trout served close to the Vltava (from which one hopes the ingredients have not been fished).

➕ E5 ✉ Rašínovo nábřeží, Nové město ☎ 29 49 64 Ⓜ Karlovo náměstí

Alive, alive o!

Cut off from the sea, Czechs have traditionally made much of freshwater fish such as trout and carp. The huge ponds constructed in the Middle Ages in which the carp in particular were bred by the thousand are still very much in use. Carp make up the traditional Christmas Eve dinner, and are bought live by sharp-eyed buyers from the equally sharp dealers who set up fish tanks in the streets and squares in the days leading up to the holiday.

INTERNATIONAL CUISINE

Beware

Since 1989, restaurants targeted at a specifically foreign clientele have multiplied in number. The temptation has been to charge international prices without providing a corresponding level of food, setting, or service. Always study your checks, and give a tip only if service has been satisfactory.

CONTINENTAL

CERBERUS ($$)

Attractive setting for Czech and continental cooking. Situated in the New Town, not far from the Municipal House (► 46).

🔲 F4 ⊠ Soukenická 19, Nové město ☎ 23 10 985 🇶 Náměstí Republiky

DAVID ($$)

An intimate setting and faultless food, including melt-in-the-mouth lamb, a house specialty.

🔲 D4 ⊠ Tržiště 21, Malá Strana ☎ 53 93 25 🇶 Malostranská 🚋 Tram 22 to Malostranské náměstí

FROM THE NEW WORLD ($$)

On the upper floor of the city's first Western-style shopping mall in suburban Vinohrady.

🔲 G5 ⊠ Vinohradská 50 ☎ 2209 7320 🇶 Náměstí miru

HANAVSKÝ PAVILON ($$)

The delightful little art-nouveau Hanava Pavilion, perched high above the River Vltava, serves mostly foreign guests.

🔲 D3 ⊠ Letenské sady 173 ☎ 32 57 92 🚋 Tram 18 to Chotkovy sady

KAMPA PARK ($$)

Stylish food in a pretty pink house on Kampa Island.

🔲 D4 ⊠ Na Kampě 8b ☎ 5731 3493 🇶 Malostranská 🚋 Tram 22 to Malostranské náměstí

KLÁŠTERNÍ VINÁRNA ($$)

Excellent steaks in the "Monastery" wine restaurant.

🔲 E5 ⊠ Národní třída 8, Nové město ☎ 29 05 96 🇶 Národní třída

LOBKOVICKÁ VINÁRNA ($$)

The cooking is imaginative in this wine restaurant run by the aristocratic Lobkovics. Features wines from the family estate at Mělník.

🔲 C4 ⊠ Vlašská 17, Malá Strana ☎ 53 01 85 🚋 Tram 22 to Malostranské náměstí

SVATÁ KLÁRA ($$)

Charcoal-grilled and flambéed specialties in the aristocratic Troja Château.

🔲 D1 ⊠ U trojského zámku 9 ☎ 688 04 05 🇶 Nádraží Holešovice then Bus 112 to Zoologická zahrada

U MODRÉ KACHNIČKY ($$)

"The Blue Duckling" was an instant success when it opened in 1993. First-rate game is served in its intimate, antiques-furnished rooms.

🔲 D4 ⊠ Nebovidská 6, Malá Strana ☎ 5732 0308 🚋 Tram 22 to Hellichova

U MODRÉ RŮŽE ($$)

In an atmospheric Old Town cellar, "The Blue Rose" serves notable fish and game.

🔲 E4 ⊠ Rytířská 16, Staré město ☎ 26 10 81 or 26 38 86 🇶 Můstek

U ZLATÉ HRUŠKY ($$$)

The "Golden Pear," in a charming rococo house in

romantic Nový svět, has an attractive outdoor section.

✚ C4 ✉ Nový svět 3, Hradčany ☎ 2051 5356
🚊 Tram 22 to Brusnice

V ZATIŠÍ ($$)

All-round excellence and sophistication just off the Royal Way. This fine restaurant (whose name means "Still Life" or "Seclusion") opened not long after the Velvet Revolution and is now a Prague institution.

✚ E4 ✉ Liliová 1, Staré město
☎ 24 22 89 77
Ⓜ Staroměstská

GRILLS

OPERA GRILL ($$$)

Fabulous food served in an intimate setting that oozes elegance.

✚ E4 ✉ Karoliny Světlé 35, Staré město ☎ 26 55 08
Ⓜ Národní třída

ROTISSERIE ($$)

Long-established grill that has maintained its standards in the face of much competition.

✚ E5 ✉ Mikulandská 6, Nové město ☎ 24 91 23 34
Ⓜ Národní třída

SEAFOOD

CANADIAN LOBSTER ($$$)

Expect to pay high prices for the impeccable fish.

✚ E4 ✉ Husova 15, Staré město ☎ 24 21 35 30
Ⓜ Národní třída or Staroměstská

REYKAVÍK ($$)

A welcome stop along the tourist trail between Old Town Square and Charles Bridge, this Icelandic establishment serves fresh fish flown in from cold North Atlantic waters.

✚ E4 ✉ Karlova 20, Staré město ☎ 2422 9251
Ⓜ Staroměstská

U VOJÁČKŮ ($$)

Good fish soups and salmon steaks not far from the Vltava in left-bank Prague.

✚ D5 ✉ Vodní 11
☎ 53 56 68 🚊 Trams 6, 9 to Kinského zahrada

AMERICAN

AVALON ($$$)

Convincing replica of an American diner set in Malá Strana Square.

✚ D4 ✉ Malostranské náměstí 12, Malá Strana
☎ 5753 0021
Ⓜ Malostranská 🚊 Tram 22 to Malostranské náměstí

BUFFALO BILL'S ($–$$)

Tacos, tortilla soup, and other Tex-Mex delicacies.

✚ E5 ✉ Vodičkova 9
☎ 2421 5479 Ⓜ Můstek

FRENCH

LA PROVENCE ($$$)

French specialties, from cassoulet to coq au vin.

✚ E4 ✉ Štupartská 9
☎ 232 48 01 Ⓜ Náměstí Republiky

U MALÍŘŮ ($$$)

The French food served in "The Painter" is sublime. In an ancient house in the middle of Malá Strana.

✚ D4 ✉ Maltézské náměstí 11, Malá Strana ☎ 5732 0317
🚊 Tram 22, 23 to Hellichova

Local fast food

Western fast food is now available in many places, but better by far (and much cheaper) for a quick snack are the local *obložené chlebíčky* (open-faced sandwiches). Each of these is like a miniature meal, perhaps consisting of a sliver or two of ham or salami and a slice of hard-boiled egg, the whole garnished with mayonnaise and topped with pieces of pickle and red pepper.

ITALIAN

BELLA NAPOLI ($–$$)

Not just Neapolitan food but other Italian delights only a short step from busy Wenceslas Square.
✚ E5 ✉ V jámě 8, Nové město ☎ 24 22 73 15 Ⓜ Muzeum

IL RITROVO ($–$$)

An amiable Florentine restaurant not far from Wenceslas Square, designed to make Italian expats feel *a casa*.
✚ F5/6 ✉ Lublaňská 11, Vinohrady ☎ 29 65 29 Ⓜ I. P. Pavlova

SEGAFREDO ESPRESSO AND TRATTORIA ($$)

Italian excitement in the old Severin Palace.
✚ E4 ✉ Na příkopě 10, Nové město ☎ 24 21 07 16 Ⓜ Můstek or Náměstí Republiky

GREEK

FAROS ($–$$)

Moussaka and other Greek specialties.
✚ C4 ✉ Šporkova 5, Malá Strana ☎ 5731 6945 Ⓜ Tram 22 to Malostranské náměstí

MIDDLE EASTERN

ADONIS ($)

A popular lunch spot offering a whole range of Middle Eastern delicacies.
✚ E5 ✉ Jungmannova 21, Nové město ☎ 26 89 08 Ⓜ Můstek or Národní třída

FAKHRELDINE ($$)

Lebanese food at a branch of this internationally famous restaurant group.

✚ F3/4 ✉ Klimentská 48, Nové město ☎ 23 27 970 Ⓜ Florenc Ⓜ Tram 3 to Těšnov

ASIAN

ASIE ($–$$)

Tasty exceptions to the sometimes bland offerings of some of Prague's Chinese restaurants make it worth the trip out to Asie in the suburb of Žižkov.
✚ G4 ✉ Seifertova 18, Žižkov ☎ 697 66 10 Ⓜ Tram 5, 9, 26 to Lipanská

PRAHA TAMURA ($$$)

Unthinkable a few years ago—an excellent Japanese restaurant in the heart of Prague's Old Town.
✚ E4 ✉ Havelská 6, Staré město ☎ 24 23 20 56 Ⓜ Můstek

SATÉ ($)

Before 1989, no Czech porker expected to end up as *satay* on a skewer, but Indonesian eating has now colonized this square in upper Hradčany.
✚ C4 ✉ Pohořelec 152/3, Hradčany ☎ 53 21 13 Ⓜ Tram 22 to Pohořelec

U ZLATÉHO HADA ($$)

Once a café, the venerable "Golden Snake" is now better known for its Chinese cuisine.
✚ E4 ✉ Karlova 18, Staré město ☎ 24 22 08 43 Ⓜ Staroměstská

Czech wines and liquor

Although little known abroad, Czech wines are surprisingly good, especially both reds and whites from Moravia, and make an interesting souvenir. Liquor is cheap and often excellent. Slivovice (plum brandy) is well known, a supposed cure for all ills, while Becherovka, prepared in Carlsbad to a secret recipe, has a unique and pungent flavor.

VEGETARIAN & SCENIC RESTAURANTS

VEGETARIAN

COUNTRY LIFE ($)
Healthy eating at a couple of central venues.

⊞ E5 ⊠ Jungmannova 1, Nové město ☎ 24 19 17 39
🚇 Národní třída or Můstek

GOVINDA VEGETARIAN CLUB ($)
An alternative Hare Krishna establishment to the U Govindy (see below), in a convenient location not far from the Municipal House (► 46).

⊞ F4 ⊠ Soukenicka 27, Nové město ☎ 2481 6016
🚇 Náměstí Republiky

RADOST CAFÉ FX ($)
Trendy café; see also.

⊞ F6 ⊠ Bělehradská 120, Vinohrady ☎ 25 12 10
🚇 I. P. Pavlova

U GOVINDY
A Hare Krishna eating-place, in the unlikely surroundings of the city's eastern suburbs. As much wholefood as you can digest. Payment is by donation.

⊞ J2 ⊠ Na hrázi 5, Palmovka ☎ 2481 6016
🚇 Palmovka

RESTAURANTS WITH A VIEW OR TERRACE

NA ZVONAŘCE ($)
Billiards and bulky Czech food with a fine view of the slopes once covered with the vineyards that gave Vinohrady its name.

⊞ F6 ⊠ Šafaříkova 1, Vinohrady ☎ 2425 2775
🚋 Tram 6, 11 to Pod Karlovem or Nuselské schody

NEBOZÍZEK ($$)
The "Little Auger" looks the other way from the Parnas (see below), from the slopes of Petřín Hill toward the center. Continental food. Reached by funicular.

⊞ C5 ⊠ Petřínské sady 411, Malá Strana ☎ 53 79 05
🚋 Funicular

PARNAS ($$$)
For that special night out. Sumptuous turn-of-the-century setting and sophisticated continental cuisine combined with an unbeatable view of the Vltava and Prague Castle (reserve a window table).

⊞ D5 ⊠ Smetanovo nábřoží 2, Staré město ☎ 0101 1901 🚇 Národní třída

RESTAURACE NA VYŠEHRADĚ ($)
With its terrace and straightforward Czech cooking, this is a good place to cool off after visiting Prague's second citadel.

⊞ E7 ⊠ Štulcova 2, Vyšehrad ☎ 24 23 92 97 🚇 Vyšehrad

U KRISTIANA ($$)
Unmemorable food but a prospect to die for. "Christian's" is aboard a barge anchored below the Smetana Embankment. Order anything and savor the view across the Vltava to Charles Bridge, Malá Strana, and the castle.

⊞ D4 ⊠ Smetanovo nábřeží, Staré město ☎ 9000 0601 or 0900 0639 🚋 Tram 17, 18 to Karlovy lázně or 6, 9, 21, 22 to Národní divadlo

Veggie revolution

Before 1989, vegetarians venturing to Prague were liable to be served endless omelets, perhaps with extra dumplings. Czechs still like their rich and hearty meat-based dishes, but waiters and others are no longer fazed when a foreigner expresses an interest in something else.

Kosher food

Reliable kosher food can be had at Kosher Restaurant Shalom ($–$$), in the former meeting room of the Jewish Town Hall.

⊞ E4 ⊠ Maislova 18, Staré město ☎ 24 81 09 29
🚇 Staroměstská

Pubs, Bars & Cafés

Czech beer

Lager beer was virtually invented in Bohemia, when the citizens of Pilsen (Plzeň) got together to form the "Burghers' Brewery" in 1842 and began producing the light and tasty liquid that has spawned endless imitation "pils" ever since but which has never been surpassed. But other Czech beers are just as good, better from the barrel than the bottle. Try Prague's own Staropramen or Braník, or the milder Budvar from České Budějovice (Budweis) in southern Bohemia.

PUBS

BRANICKÁ FORMANKA

The suburban Braník brewery is one of four major breweries in Prague. This pub is its downtown outlet.

✚ E5 ⊠ Vodičkova 26, Nové město ☎ 2421 7103 Ⓜ Můstek

ČERNÝ PIVOVAR

The taps at the "Black Brewery" are constantly pulling up dark beer for the crowds in this no-frills Charles Square establishment.

✚ E5 ⊠ Karlovo náměstí 15, Nové město Ⓜ Karlovo náměstí

JAMES JOYCE

Guinness and other Irish beers—should you tire of the wonders of Czech beer. Largely expatriate crowd.

✚ E4 ⊠ Liliová 10, Staré město Ⓜ Staroměstská

NOVOMĚSTSKÝ PIVOVAR

The New Town Brewery is Prague's other boutique brewery (after U Fleků), and is housed in a medieval building.

✚ E5 ⊠ Vodičkova 20, Nové město Ⓜ Můstek

U FLEKŮ

Every visitor should sip the dark and tasty beer that has been brewed and served on these raucous premises for 200 years. There's also a big beer garden.

✚ E5 ⊠ Křemencova 11, Nové město ☎ 24 91 51 18 Ⓜ Karlovo náměstí or Národní třída

U KOCOURA

The famous old "Tomcat" is a welcome sight on the hard trek up from Malá Strana to Prague Castle.

✚ D4 ⊠ Nerudova 2, Malá Strana Ⓜ Tram 22 to Malostranské náměstí

U MEDVÍDKŮ

Budvar, from the town of České Budějovice in southern Bohemia, is probably the best-known Bohemian beer apart from Pilsener. Try it here on tap—out in the garden in summer.

✚ E4 ⊠ Na Perštýně 7, Staré město Ⓜ Národní třída

U SVATÉHO TOMÁŠE

The monks no longer brew their own here, but medieval St. Thomas's is a popular stop for tour groups. Folk-music performances.

✚ D4 ⊠ Letenská 12, Malá Strana Ⓜ Malostranská

U VEJVODŮ

Don't be put off by the scruffy appearance; this is one of the most ancient and authentic of Prague's downtown pubs, with the local Staropramen brew on tap.

✚ E4 ⊠ Jilská 4, Staré město ☎ 24 21 05 91 Ⓜ Národní třída

U ZLATÉHO TYGRA

Perfect Pilsener, drawn straight from the 13th-century cellars of the "Golden Tiger," has long made this pub a favorite with serious local drinkers.

✚ E4 ⊠ Husova 17, Staré město ☎ 24 22 90 20 Ⓜ Staroměstská

CAFÉS & BARS

ARCHA

This café, next to one of the country's biggest publishing houses, attracts a youthful, intellectual set.

➕ F4 ✉ Na poříčí 26, north Nové město ☎ 232 41 49 Ⓜ Náměstí Republiky

CAFÉ MILENA

Another elegant café in Old Town Square.

➕ E4 ✉ Staroměstské náměstí 22, Staré město ☎ 26 08 43 Ⓜ Staroměstská

CAFÉ SAVOY

Refined turn-of-the-century café at the Malá Strana end of the Legions' Bridge (Most legií).

➕ D5 ✉ Vítězná 5, Malá Strana ☎ 53 50 00 🚃 Tram 6, 9, 22 to Újezd

CAFFÈ DANTE

Streamlined Italian café opposite the modern art collections of the Trades Fair Palace.

➕ F3 ✉ Dukelských hrdinů 16, Holešovice ☎ 87 01 93 🚃 Tram 5, 12, 17 to Veletržní

DOLCE VITA

Authentic espresso close to Old Town Square.

➕ E4 ✉ Široká 15, Staré město Ⓜ Staroměstská

EVROPA

In spite of the arrogance of charging an entrance fee, the art-nouveau café of the Evropa Hotel is not to be missed.

➕ E5 ✉ Václavské náměstí 25, Nové město ☎ 24 22 81 17 Ⓜ Můstek

GULU GULU

You'll be lucky to get a table at this hip spot in Bethlehem Square, which buzzes like a beehive until midnight.

➕ E4 ✉ Betlémské náměstí 8, Staré město ☎ 9001 2581 Ⓜ Národní třída

INSTITUT FRANÇAIS

Pleasant French café in the New Town just off Wenceslas Square.

➕ E5 ✉ Štěpánská 35, Nové město ☎ 24 21 40 32 Ⓜ Můstek or Muzeum

SLAVIA

This classic Central European café, with its view over the Vltava, is open again after a long and controversial period of closure.

➕ D5 ✉ Smetanovo nábřeží 2, Staré město ☎ 2422 0957 Ⓜ Národní třída

VELRYBA

The "Whale" opens wide its jaws to accommodate its trendy clientele.

➕ E5 ✉ Opatovická 24, Nové město ☎ 2491 2484 Ⓜ Národní třída

Turkish coffee

Espresso, cappuccino, and most other coffees can now be found in Prague, but don't be surprised if you get served a traditional *"turecká káva."* This is Turkish coffee, fine when you're accustomed to it and know when to stop swallowing—that is before you disturb the deposit of coffee grounds at the bottom of the cup.

Books & Antiques

Bargains... perhaps

Czechs are great readers, and until recently new and secondhand books were very inexpensive, many of them in languages other than Czech. Prices have risen considerably since 1989, but there are still many bargains. That said, prices for antique books are now well in line with those on the international market.

NEW BOOKS

ALBATROS
Children's books—and Czech authors and illustrators stand out in the field.
🚇 E4 ✉ Havelská 20, Staré město ☎ 2422 9322
Ⓜ Můstek

CIZOJAZYČNÁ LITERATURA
Has fair-sized stocks of what its name ("Foreign-language Literature") implies and much else.
🚇 E4 ✉ Na příkopě 27, Staré město ☎ 26 28 37 Ⓜ Můstek

FRANZ KAFKA
Stocks an excellent range of both new and secondhand books, mostly in German.
🚇 D4 ✉ U lužického semináře 19, Malá Strana ☎ 53 15 52
Ⓜ Malostranská

THE GLOBE BOOKSTORE AND COFFEEHOUSE
A congenial home-away-from-home for Americans and anyone hungry for literature in English, as well as bagels and American-style coffee. The Globe is in the inner-city suburb of Holešovice, on the north bank of the Vltava, easy to reach by public transportation.
🚇 F2 ✉ Janovského 14, near Strossmayerovo náměstí, Holešovice ☎ 66 71 26 10
🚊 Tram 5, 12, 17 to Strossmayerovo náměstí

KANZELSBERGER
Good selection of new titles, including children's stories and books on Prague and the Czech Republic, many in languages other than Czech.
🚇 E5 ✉ Václavské náměstí (Wenceslas Square) 42, Nové město ☎ 24 21 73 35
Ⓜ Můstek

KIWI
Don't be put off by the travel agency on the ground floor; the shop in the basement has one of the best selections of maps and guides in town.
🚇 E5 ✉ Jungmannova 23, Nové město ☎ 2423 4756
Ⓜ Národní třída

KNIHKUPECTVÍ NA MŮSTKU
A famous-name bookstore with an excellent selection of maps.
🚇 E4 ✉ Na příkopě 3, Staré město ☎ 2421 6383
Ⓜ Můstek

KNIHKUPECTVÍ U ČERNÉ MATKY BOŽÍ
A large, well-stocked bookstore that carries virtually every foreign-language title published locally, as well as a good range of travel books and maps. Unmissable location in the Cubist House at the Black Madonna (► 56).
🚇 E4 ✉ Celetná 34, Staré město ☎ 2421 1155
Ⓜ Náměstí Republiky

U KNIHOMOLA
An enticing new basement bookshop, "The Bookworm" attempts to supply the fullest possible range of foreign-language volumes. The even deeper basement café with periodicals to read is a bonus.
🚇 G5 ✉ Mánesova 79, Vinohrady ☎ 627 77 70
Ⓜ Jiřího z Poděbrad

ANTIQUES & ANTIQUARIAN BOOKSTORES

ANTIKVARIÁT EVA KOZÁKOVÁ
Old photographs, prints, and postcards, plus innumerable old books, mostly Czech.
✚ E5 ✉ Myslíkova 10, Nové město ☎ 29 44 02
Ⓜ Karlovo náměstí

ANTIKVARIÁT GALERIE MŮSTEK
Printed treasures of all kinds in a spacious Old Town basement. Many engravings, maps, and even paintings.
✚ E4 ✉ 28 října 13, Staré město ☎ 26 80 58 Ⓜ Můstek

ANTIKVARIÁT KAREL KŘENEK
Refined establishment near the start of the Royal Way, with an excellent range of prints and watercolors as well as fine old books.
✚ E4 ✉ Celetná 31, Staré město ☎ 231 47 34
Ⓜ Náměstí Republiky

ANTIKVARIÁT NA VALDŠTEJNSKÉM NÁMĚSTÍ
The Malá Strana mecca for lovers of old books.
✚ D4 ✉ Valdštejnské náměstí 7, Malá Strana
Ⓜ Malostranská

ANTIKVARIÁT U KARLOVA MOSTU
Fine old books and printed memorabilia of all kinds. Not particularly cheap.
✚ E4 ✉ Karlova 2, Staré město ☎ 24 22 92 05
Ⓜ Staroměstská

DOROTHEUM
This branch of the long-established Vienna auction-house has a fine range of antiques of all kinds. No bargains, but no rip-offs either.
✚ E4 ✉ Ovocný trh, Staré město ☎ 24 22 20 01
Ⓜ Můstek or Náměstí Republiky

GALERIE LUKAŠ
Exquisite objects of international as well as Czech origin.
✚ E5 ✉ Národní třída 21, Nové město ☎ 24 21 33 38
Ⓜ Národní třída

PRAŽSKÉ STAROŽITNOSTI
"Prague Antiques" sells jewelry, porcelain, and paintings galore.
✚ E5 ✉ Mikulandská 8, Nové město ☎ 29 41 70
Ⓜ Národní třída

VLADIMIR ANDRLE
This antiques shop, in Wenceslas Square, is a handy starting point during your hunt for collectables.
✚ E5 ✉ Václavské náměstí 17, Nové město ☎ 2400 9166
Ⓜ Můstek

ZLATÁ KORUNA
Antique coins, medals, and paper money.
✚ E4 ✉ Pařížská 8, Staré město ☎ 231 32 85
Ⓜ Staroměstská

Wenceslas Hollar

One of the first artists to make accurate drawings of the English landscape was Wenceslas Hollar. Born in 1607 in Bohemia, Václav (to give him his Czech name) sought refuge abroad following the Protestant defeat at the Battle of the White Mountain, and was employed as a draftsman by the Earl of Arundel. A trawl through Prague's antiquarian bookstores might turn up a Hollar original, such as his wonderfully detailed 1636 panorama of the city, but there are plenty of alternatives by other artists—drawings, engravings, and maps—at affordable prices.

GIFTS, SOUVENIRS & MUSIC

Kafka at home

One of the many places lived in by novelist Franz Kafka was the house on Celetná Street adjoining Týn Church. In the bedroom in which Kafka slept and dreamed as a child, a blank window faces down the south aisle of the church's nave.

Sgraffito

The Schwarzenberg Palace on Hradčany Square is probably Prague's most splendidly sgraffitoed building. Sgraffito work involves picking out patterns in two shades of plasterwork either to accentuate the architectural character of the building, or to cover the façade with lively pictures (as in the Martinic Palace, also in Hradčany Square).

TOYS, PUPPETS & SOUVENIRS

ALBATROS
The place for soft toys as well as children's books.
✚ E4 ✉ Havelská 20, Staré město ☎ 2422 9322 🚇 Můstek

ČESKÝ NÁRODNÍ PODNIK
Folksy artifacts include Christmas creches as well as willow whips with which to harass village maidens at Eastertime.
✚ E4 ✉ Husova 12, Staré město ☎ 24 21 08 86 🚇 Staroměstská

DIVADELNÍ KNIHKUPECTVÍ A LOUTKY
Looking for a puppet as a souvenir? "Theater Bookstore and Marionettes" sells hand-made marionettes of superior quality to those available on the street at correspondingly higher prices. Worth visiting if only to study the several kinds of Devil that play such a prominent part in Czech puppetry.
✚ E4 ✉ Celetná 17, Staré město 🚇 Náměstí Republiky

DŘEVENÉ HRAČKY
Sensible and imaginative wooden toys.
✚ E4 ✉ Karlova 26, Staré město 🚇 Staroměstská

EXPOZICE FRANZE KAFKY
Prague's most famous writer must have spun around in his grave many times at the souvenir industry, which has impressed his haggard features on countless T-shirts. This has the least tacky selection of Kafkeriana in the city.
✚ E4 ✉ Corner of Maislova and Kaprova, Staré město 🚇 Staroměstská

KROKODIL
New and secondhand trains galore, including rarities dating from the Communist era.
✚ D5 ✉ Bartolomějská 3, Staré město 🚇 Národní třída

LIŠKA
Central Europeans still wear their furs without shame, purchased from elegant outlets such as "The Fox" near Old Town Square. If you're on a budget, look instead for fox-fur hats at bargain prices in the Havelská market.
✚ E4 ✉ Železná 1, Staré město 🚇 Staroměstská

MUSEUM SHOP
Unusually tasteful and original souvenirs based on the treasures of the many Prague museums, plus foreign art books not available elsewhere in Prague. An example to other souvenir shops worldwide; where else, for example, could you buy a china mug with elegant sgraffito patterning?
✚ D4 ✉ Jiřská 6, Hradčany ☎ 2437 3255 🚊 Tram 22 to Pražský hrad

OBCHOD S LOUTKAMI
Another place to find a plethora of puppetry.
✚ C4 ✉ Nerudova 47, Malá Strana 🚊 Tram 22 to Malostranské náměstí

ARTS & CRAFTS

CRISTALLINO
Designer glassware, a Czech specialty.
⊞ E4 ✉ Celetná 12, Staré město ☎ 24 21 48 52 Ⓜ Náměstí Republiky.
Also at
⊞ E4 ✉ Celetná 19, Staré město ☎ 26 12 65 Ⓜ Náměstí Republiky

CRYSTAL
Wonderfully decorated glass from Nový Bor in northern Bohemia.
⊞ E4 ✉ Karlova 21, 24, Staré město ☎ 25 46 25 Ⓜ Staroměstská

GALERIE DOMINO
Czech and Slovak applied arts
⊞ C3 ✉ Wuchterlova 14, Dejvice ☎ 2431 7659 Ⓜ Dejvická

GALERIE PEITHNER-LICHTENFELS
Modern Czech and Austrian art, including works from the period between the wars.
⊞ E4 ✉ Michalská 12, Staré město ☎ 24 22 76 80 Ⓜ Můstek

GRANÁT
Bohemian garnets are world-famous; this shop has the most varied selection.
⊞ E4 ✉ Dlouhá 30, Staré město ☎ 231 5612 Ⓜ Náměstí Republiky

MOSER
The outlet for the fine crystal and porcelain made in Carlsbad (Karlovy vary), plus porcelain from Meissen and Herend.
⊞ E4 ✉ Na příkopě 12, Staré město ☎ 24 21 12 93 Ⓜ Můstek or Náměstí Republiky

SKLO BOHEMIA
Bohemian glassware from Světlá nad Sázavou.
⊞ E4 ✉ Na příkopě 17 ☎ 24 21 05 74 Ⓜ Můstek or Náměstí Republiky

MUSIC

AGHARTA
Jazz, jazz, and more jazz on sale at this nightspot.
⊞ F5 ✉ Krakovská 5, Nové město 🕐 Evenings only Ⓜ Muzeum

BONTONLAND KORUNA
Reputedly the biggest music store in Central Europe, although better for pop and rock than classical music. In the labyrinthine basement of the Koruna Palace at the corner of Wenceslas Square and Na příkopě.
⊞ E4 ✉ Václavské náměstí 1, Nové město ☎ 2423 5356 Ⓜ Můstek

POPRON
CDs and tapes galore.
⊞ E5 ✉ Jungmannova 30, Nové město Ⓜ Národní třída or Můstek

Musical miscellany

In addition to excellent discs of music by the classical composers most closely associated with the city (Mozart, Dvořák, Smetana...), Prague stores stock strongly flavored and highly individual pop music (Šum Svistu, or Laura and her Tigers, Support Lesbians, Shalom...). Even more distinctive are the brass bands—the best you've ever heard—pumping out Czech (yes, Czech) old-time favorites such as "Roll Out the Barrel" ("*Škoda lásky*").

73

DEPARTMENT STORES, MARKETS & FOOD

Red Army surplus

After 1989, the Warsaw Pact crumbled and the Red Army began its long retreat back to Moscow, shedding its surplus equipment as it went. Many Czech farmers now carry a Kalashnikov rather than a humble shotgun, while visitors may still find themselves tempted by the trim greatcoats or the improbably high-peaked officers' caps that are on sale wherever tourists congregate.

DEPARTMENT STORES

BILÁ LABUŤ
The "White Swan" is a long-established department store on an unfashionable but interesting shopping street just east of the Old Town (a smaller branch is now open on Wenceslas Square opposite the National Museum).
✚ F4 ✉ Na Poříčí 23, north Nové město Ⓜ Náměstí Republiky

KOTVA
The "Anchor" was completed in 1975 and for a while was the city's foremost shopping site, though the range of goods would have seemed basic to Western consumers. Nowadays, though the anodized aluminum and tinted glass exterior remains as intimidating as ever, it is full of fine things from all over the world.
✚ E4 ✉ Náměstí Republiky 8, Staré město Ⓜ Náměstí Republiky

TESCO
Rival to Kotva, and once bearing the impeccably proletarian name of "Máj" (May), this department store is now in British hands. A ride up the escalator gives a good view of the downtown scene.
✚ E5 ✉ Národní 26, Nové město Ⓜ Národní třída

KRONE
A German equivalent of Tesco, on Wenceslas Square.
✚ E4 ✉ Václavské náměstí 21 Ⓜ Můstek

MARKETS

HAVELSKÁ/ V KOTCÍCH
Atmospheric market for fruits, vegetables, and souvenirs.
✚ E4 ✉ Staré město Ⓒ Daily Ⓜ Můstek

PRAGUE MARKET
Comprehensive market on the far side of the Vltava, north of Old Town.
✚ G3 ✉ Bubenské nábřeží, Holešovice Ⓒ Daily Ⓜ Vltavská

PRAŽSKÁ BURZA
Cheap clothes, motor parts, and an abundance of things you won't want— but a fascinating spectacle none the less.
✚ F2 ✉ Výstaviště (Exhibition Grounds), Holešovice Ⓒ Sat–Sun 9–12 Ⓜ Holešovice 🚋 Tram 5, 12, 17

FOOD SHOPS

COUNTRY LIFE
Healthy natural foods that are difficult to obtain in this calorie-addicted city.
✚ E4 ✉ Melantrichova 15, Staré město Ⓜ Můstek

FRUITS DE FRANCE
"French Fruits" changed the face of food shopping in Prague not long after the Velvet Revolution, and is still the place for classy imported foods.
✚ E4 ✉ Jindřišská 9, Nové město Ⓜ Můstek

UZENINY
Every kind of Central European sausage.
✚ E5 ✉ Václavské náměstí 34 Ⓜ Můstek

OPERA & CLASSICAL MUSIC

OPERA

ESTATES THEATER (STAVOVSKÉ DIVADLO)

The venue that saw the premiere of Mozart's *Don Giovanni* in 1787 is a marvel of pristine neoclassical glory. Regular performances of Wolfgang's greatest hits.

✚ E4 ✉ Ovocný trh, Staré město ☎ 24 21 50 01 or 26 77 97 Ⓜ Můstek

NATIONAL THEATER (NÁRODNÍ DIVADLO)

Operas from both the Czech and international repertoire in a sumptuous setting.

➤ 36

STATE OPERA

Opened in 1887 as the Deutsches Theater (German Theater), this neo-Renaissance building became the Smetana Theater (Smetanovo divadlo) after World War II. It's now the State Opera, with performances from the international repertoire and classical ballet.

✚ F5 ✉ Wilsonova 4, Nové město ☎ 24 22 76 93. Box office: 26 53 53 Ⓜ Muzeum

CLASSICAL MUSIC

BERTRAMKA

The villa of Mozart's Prague patrons is now a museum and chamber-concert hall.

➤ 57

HOUSE AT THE STONE BELL (DŮM U KAMMANÉHO ZVONU)

Contemporary classical compositions augment the traditional repertoire in this Gothic mansion on Old Town Square.

✚ E4 ✉ Staroměstské náměstí 13, Staré město ☎ 2482 7526 Ⓜ Staroměstská

KLEMENTINUM

Chamber concerts in the Hall of Mirrors (Zrcadlová síň) of this vast complex.

✚ E4 ✉ Křižovnické náměstí, Staré město ☎ 2422 9500 Ⓜ Staroměstská

LIECHTENSTEIN PALACE (LICHTENSTEJNSKÝ PALÁC)

Palatial setting for symphonic and other performances.

✚ D4 ✉ Malostranské náměstí 13, Malá Strana ☎ 53 09 43 Ⓜ Staroměstská 🚃 Tram 22 to Malostranské náměstí

LOBKOVIC PALACE (LOBKOVICKÝ PALÁC)

Chamber concerts in the banqueting hall of a palace in the castle precinct.

✚ D4 ✉ Jiřská 3, Hradčany ☎ 53 73 06 Ⓜ Malostranská then uphill walk 🚃 Tram 22 to Pražský hrad

NOSTIC PALACE (NOSTICKÝ PALÁC)

Count Nostic was the founder of the Estates Theater. His own palace makes a fine setting for chamber concerts.

✚ D4 ✉ Maltézské náměstí 1, Malá Strana ☎ 5731 1590 🚃 Tram 22 to Hellichova

RUDOLFINUM

This splendid neo-Renaissance hall on the banks of the Vltava is the

Mozart in Prague

"My Praguers understand me," declared Mozart, who was far better received here than in Vienna. Both *Figaro* and *Don Giovanni* were hits in Prague, and after his pauper's death in Vienna, it was Prague that honored him with a great funeral mass in Malá Strana's St. Nicholas' Church, attended by a crowd of 4,000 mourners.

Josef Kajetán Tyl

The Estates Theater (Stavovské divadlo; ➤ 75) reverted to its original name in 1991. For many years it was called the Tyl Theater; almost unknown abroad, the 19th-century playwright Josef Kajetán Tyl is dear to Czech hearts for his comedy *Fidlovačka*, which contains the song *"Kde domov můj?"* ('Where is my home?'), a plaintive call that later formed the first line of the Czechoslovak national anthem.

home of the Czech Philharmonic Orchestra, which performs in the big Dvořák Hall. The Little (or Suk) Hall is used for chamber concerts.

✚ E4 ✉ Alšovo nábřeží 12, Staré město ☎ 24 89 33 52 Ⓜ Staroměstská

ST. AGNES'S CONVENT (ANEŽSKÝ KLÁŠTER)

Chamber music in one of the convent's two churches.
➤ 41

ST. GEORGE'S BASILICA (BAZILIKA SVATÉHO JIŘÍ)

The castle's austere Romanesque church is now used for chamber concerts.
➤ 31

ST. JAMES'S CHURCH (KOSTEL SVATÉHO JAKUBA)

The admirable acoustics in this Old Town church augment the concerts of sacred music held here.
➤ 55

ST. NICHOLAS'S CHURCH (CHRÁM SVATÉHO MIKULÁŠE), MALÁ STRANA

The organ that Mozart played in Prague's greatest Baroque church still accompanies choral concerts.
➤ 33

ST. NICHOLAS'S CHURCH, OLD TOWN (CHRÁM SVATÉHO MIKULÁŠE, STARÉ MĚSTO)

The other Church of St. Nicholas is less

sumptuous than the one in Malá Strana but an equally fine choice for organ and vocal recitals.
➤ 55

SMETANA HALL (SMETANOVA SÍŇ)

Part of the sumptuously decorated and recently renovated Municipal House, and home of the Czech Symphony Orchestra.
➤ 57

TROJA CHÂTEAU (TROJSKÝ ZÁMEK)

The magnificence of Count Šternberg's out-of-town palace almost overwhelms the music.
➤ 48

VILA AMERIKA

Evenings, Count Michna's jolly little 18th-century summer palace, home of the Dvořák Museum, stages tributes to the composer's life and work.
➤ 57

WALLENSTEIN PALACE (VALDŠTEJNSKÝ PALÁC)

Wonderful summer evening concerts in the Baroque gardens of the palace.
➤ 34

JAZZ, POP & NIGHTLIFE

POP & ROCK

BORAT
Grimy, noisy haunt that appeals to some.

✠ D4 ✉ Újezd 18 ☎ 53 83 62 🚃 Tram 22 to Hellichova

BOTEL ADMIRÁL
Disco on the deck aboard one of Prague's floating hotels.

✠ D6 ✉ Hořejší nábřeži, Smichov ☎ 5732 1302 Ⓜ Karlovo náměstí then cross Palacky Bridge

LÁVKA
Come here for dancing to recorded music on the riverside close to Prague's most celebrated bridge, Karlův most (Charles Bridge).

✠ D4 ✉ Novotného lávka 1, Staré město ☎ 24 21 47 97 Ⓜ Staroměstská

LUCERNA MUSIC BAR
This is part of the vast complex of the Lucerna Palace, a labyrinth of arcades and passageways that were the work of President Havel's builder-grandfather. Its good-sized ballroom can accommodate visiting groups as well as locals, and although some expats look down on it, it's the place to go for Czech retro.

✠ E5 ✉ Vodičkova 36, Nové město ☎ 2421 7108 Ⓜ Můstek

MALOSTRANSKÁ BESEDA
Something for everyone— ska, folk, reggae, and blues, as well as rock. You might even catch the Prague Syncopators,

with their immaculate re-creation of vintage swing. Before or after the music you can relax in the café-cum-gallery that also occupies the premises.

✠ D4 ✉ Malostranské náměstí 21, Malá Strana ☎ 53 90 24 Ⓜ Malostranská 🚃 Tram 22 to Malostranské náměstí

MUSIC PARK
Not the place for claustrophobes. You'll never be alone, least of all on a Saturday night, in this biggest and most popular of all the city's dance clubs. Two Metro stops east of Wenceslas Square.

✠ F6 ✉ Francouzská 4, Vinohrady ☎ 69 11 768 Ⓜ Náměstí Míru

RADOST FX
Disco plus occasional live music east of the downtown area.

✠ F6 ✉ Bělehradská 120, Vinohrady ☎ 2425 4776 Ⓜ I. P. Pavlova

ROCK CAFÉ
This downtown café and concert spot is the place to go if you like your rock both hard and very loud.

✠ E5 ✉ Národní 20, Nové město ☎ 2491 4414 Ⓜ Národní třída

ROXY
Unusual underground establishment that makes its point with videos as well as music. Funk and techno dominate.

✠ E4 ✉ Dlouhá 33, Staré město ☎ 2481 0951 Ⓜ Staroměstská

Rock Czech-style

Before 1989, groups like the Plastic People of the Universe were seen as genuinely subversive of the existing order and were relentlessly hounded by State Security. Nowadays, the rock scene is a confused one, with a lot of fairly mindless imitation of Western trends but some innovation too, by groups like Šum Svistu (Latin influenced) and Shalom (obsessed by Judaism).

Prague jazz

Jazz has deep roots among the Czech people, as evidenced in the novels and short stories of the long-exiled writer Josef Škvorecký (for example *The Bass Saxophone*). The Prague jazz scene is highly concentrated, with the majority of venues closely clustered in the area between the National Theater and Wenceslas Square.

JAZZ

AGHARTA JAZZ CENTRUM

Cramped but enjoyable for local and international jazz, with cocktails and snacks. CD shop.

⊞ F5 ✉ Krakovská 5, Nové město ☎ 2221 1275 Ⓜ Muzeum

JAZZ CLUB U STARÉ PANÍ

Some of the best local musicians play in this central jazz club.

⊞ E4 ✉ Michalská 9, Staré město ☎ 26 49 20 Ⓜ Můstek

JAZZ CLUB ŽELEZNÁ

Another minuscule club for jazzers, this one in ancient cellars in the heart of the Old Town. The music is mostly trad, of the kind played on the tourist trail during the day.

⊞ E4 ✉ Železná 16, Staré město ☎ 2423 9697 Ⓜ Můstek

METROPOLITAN

Swing, ragtime, and blues.

⊞ E5 ✉ Jungmannova 14, Nové město ☎ 24 21 60 25 Ⓜ Národní třída

REDUTA

Bill Clinton blew his sax at this best-known of Prague jazz locales during the presidential visit to Prague. You can hear Dixieland, swing, and modern jazz.

⊞ E5 ✉ Národní 20, Nové město ☎ 24 91 22 46 Ⓜ Národní třída

U MALÉHO GLENA

"Little Glenn's" is named after its genial American owner, who provides recorded jazz in the candlelit upstairs bar and the real thing—alternating with pop and rock—in the tiny basement.

⊞ D4 ✉ Karmelitská 23, Malá Strana ☎ 535 8115 🚋 Tram 12, 22

VIOLA

Saturday night events only.

⊞ E5 ✉ Národní třída 7, Nové město ☎ 24 22 08 44 Ⓜ Národní třída

CASINOS & CABARETS

If you want to see a good old-fashioned floor show, with music, dancing, and spectacle, the larger hotels are the best bet. Advance booking is essential.

CASINO BLUE DIAMOND

Roulette and other games, played in spacious modern surroundings in Prague's biggest hotel.

⊞ F3 ✉ Hotel Atrium, Pobřežní 1, Karlín ☎ 24 84 20 05 Ⓜ Florenc

CASINO PALAIS SAVARIN

Roulette and other games of chance.

⊞ E4 ✉ Na příkopě 10, Nové město ☎ 24 22 16 36 Ⓜ Můstek or Náměstí Republiky

VARIETÉ PRAGA

Variety, brass bands, and gaming in a wonderful building in art-nouveau style.

⊞ E5 ✉ Vodičkova 30, Nové město ☎ 2421 5945 Ⓜ Můstek

MOVIES & THEATER

MOVIES

Prague has dozens of movie theaters, many around Wenceslas Square. Recent releases are often shown in the original version with Czech subtitles.

THEATER

You don't have to speak Czech to enjoy mime and multimedia (known locally as "Black Light" theater), big on the Prague stage. Most such shows are devised for foreign visitors.

ARCHA THEATER

Varied program, designed to appeal to the visitor from abroad.

✚ F4 ✉ Na poříčí 26, north Nové město ☎ 232 75 70
Ⓜ Náměstí Republiky

CELETNÁ THEATER

Shows are designed for summer visitors eager to hear more about the life and times of Prague's literary giant, Franz Kafka.

✚ E4 ✉ Celetná 17, Staré město ☎ 24 81 27 62
Ⓜ Náměstí Republiky

IMAGE THEATER (DIVADLO IMAGE)

Another visitor-oriented theater with "Black Light" shows, which feature dance, mime, music—you name it!

✚ E4 ✉ Pařížská 4, Staré město ☎ 232 91 91
Ⓜ Staroměstská

JIŘÍ SRNEC BLACK THEATER

Legends of magic Prague presented in multimedia

format as at the Image Theater.

✚ E5 ✉ Lucerna, Štěpánská 61, Nové město ☎ 9004 9434
Ⓜ Národní třída

KARLÍN MUSICAL THEATER (HUDEBNÍ DIVADLO V KARLÍNĚ)

Operettas and musicals are the undemanding fare in this theater in an inner suburb.

✚ F4 ✉ Křižíkova 10, Karlín ☎ 2186 8149
Ⓜ Florenc

LATERNA MAGIKA

The Magic Lantern's synthesis of film, music, theater, and mime was first developed in the 1950s by Alfréd Radok, and continues to intrigue and delight audiences. Some of the most successful shows are reworkings of ancient myths, such as Theseus and the Minotaur or the *Odyssey*.

✚ D/E5 ✉ Nová scéna of the National Theater, Národní třída 2, Nové město ☎ 24 91 41 29
Ⓜ Národní třída

NATIONAL THEATRE (NÁRODNÍ DIVADLO)

You can see classics of Czech theater here, as well as performances of opera and ballet.

✚ D/E5 ✉ Národní třída 2, Nové město ☎ 24 91 34 37
Ⓜ Národní třída

ROKOKO

Some non-Czech performances are put on in this establishment in Wenceslas Square.

✚ E5 ✉ Václavské náměstí 38, Nové město ☎ 24 21 71 13
Ⓜ Můstek

Keeping you posted

Since 1989 there has been a boom in performances of all kinds intended to appeal to foreign visitors. Posters and leaflets will keep you up to date as to what's on, as will the English-language *Prague Post* weekly newspaper.

Czech puppetry

In a country where the art of manipulating marionettes is taught in universities, no one whose imagination has been stimulated by the array of delightful little figures on sale on stalls and in shops should miss one of Prague's puppet performances. The colorful characters are mostly drawn from the fairy tales that are such a feature of Czech popular literature. They include water sprites and witches, devils, soldiers and highwaymen, villains, and virgins.

TA FANTASTIKA

Another spectacle based on the Black Light fusion of dance, mime, and music—a spinoff from the hugely successful Laterna Magika.

E4 ✉ Karlova 8, Staré město ☎ 2423 7763
Ⓜ Staroměstská

THEATER ON THE BALUSTRADE (DIVADLO NA ZÁBRADLÍ)

Václav Havel shifted scenery here, and his later plays helped build the theater's reputation.

E4 ✉ Anenské náměstí 5, Staré město ☎ 24 22 95 17. Box office: 24 22 19 33 or 24 22 95 17 Ⓜ Staroměstská

PUPPETRY & FOLKLORE

CZECH FOLKLORE ENSEMBLE (ČESKÝ SOUBOR PÍSNÍ A TANCŮ)

Well-rehearsed rustic song and dance, plus operettas.

D4 ✉ Divadlo na Klárově (Klarov Theater), nábřeží E. Beneše 3, Malá Strana ☎ 53 98 37 Ⓜ Malostranská

DIVADLO MIMŮ

Pantomime in the suburbs.

F3 ✉ Františka křížka 36, Holešovice ☎ 2057 1584
🚊 Tram 5, 12, 17

MINOR THEATER (DIVADLO MINOR)

Live theater for children, as well as puppetry, in continuous performances.

F4 ✉ Senovážné náměstí 28, Nové město ☎ 24 22 96 75
Ⓜ Náměstí Republiky

NATIONAL MARIONETTE THEATER (NÁRODNÍ DIVADLO MARIONET)

Adaptations of operas are among the attractions. Matinees.

E4 ✉ Žatecká 1, Staré město ☎ 232 34 29
Ⓜ Staroměstská

SPEJBL AND HURVÍNEK THEATER (DIVADLO SPEJBLA A HURVÍNKA)

Don't miss the antics of Prague's immortal puppet duo: Josef Skupa's troubled father and his perky son have been performing in their own theater since 1945.

C3 ✉ Dejvická 38 ☎ 2431 6784 Ⓜ Dejvická

Sports & Outdoor Activities

SOCCER

SPARTA STADIUM
First-class soccer at the home of one of the country's leading teams, Sparta.

✚ E3 ✉ Milady Horákové 98 ☎ 2057 0323 🚊 Tram 26 to Sparta

ICE HOCKEY

SPARTA PRAHA
This big indoor hall is the base of H. C. Sparta Praha.

✚ F2 ✉ Výstaviště (Exhibition Grounds), Holešovice ☎ 872 7477 🚇 Holešovice

SKATING

SPORTS HALL
One of several indoor ice rinks in Prague. In winter there's also skating on ponds, lakes, and reservoirs on the outskirts of Prague.

✚ F2 ✉ Exhibition Grounds (Výstaviště), Holešovice ☎ 37 11 42 🚇 Nádraží Holešovice 🚊 Tram 5, 12, 17 to Výstaviště

SWIMMING

HOSTIVAŘ RESERVOIR
Prague's biggest reservoir; there are windsurfing and boating opportunities, as well as swimming.

✚ Off map, 7.5 miles southeast of Prague 🚇 Háje, then walk or Bus 165, 170, 212, 213

PODOLÍ POOLS (PLAVECKÝ STADION PODOLÍ)
Large complex of pools, sauna, etc.

✚ E8 ✉ Podolská 74, Podolí ☎ 61 21 43 43 🚊 Tram 3, 17 to Kublov

SLAPY DAM & LAKE
The Vltava upstream from Prague has been dammed to form a chain of lakes with beaches made of imported sand.

✚ Off map, 20 miles south of Prague 🚌 Bus from Anděl bus station

BIKING

LANDA
One of the few places in Prague to rent bikes.

✚ G5 ✉ Šumavská 33, Vinohrady ☎ 2425 6121 🚇 Náměstí Míru 🚊 Tram 16 to Šumavská

HORSE RACING

CHUCHLE RACECOURSE (ZÁVODIŠTĚ CHUCHLE)
Flat races and trotting.

✚ Off map, 6 miles south of Prague ☎ 54 30 91, 54 04 06, or 54 66 10 🚈 Suburban train from Smíchov to Velká Chuchle 🚌 Bus 172

GOLF

KARLŠTEJN
One of a number of newish courses; this one has the benefit of Karlštejn Castle (➤ 20) as a backdrop.

✚ Off map, 20 miles to the southwest ☎ 0204 67 27 27

ŠTIŘÍN CHÂTEAU (ZÁMEK ŠTIŘÍN)
This impeccably restored country house hotel has a golf course in its park.

✚ Off map, 20 miles to the southeast ☎ 0311 68 47 16

In-town biking
Bicycling is not particularly popular in this fume- and cobble-ridden city. On weekends urban bicyclists congregate in the city's extensive Stromovka Park, where there is a network of marked bike paths and some signposting indicating how bikers might reach other parts of Prague in relative safety.

81

HOTELS BY DISTRICT

Prices
Expect to pay per night for a double room
$$$ Kč4,500 +
$$ Kč2,000–4,500
$ Kč1,000–2,000

HRADČANY & LESSER TOWN (MALÁ STRANA)

The castle quarter and the "Lesser Town" between the castle and the River Vltava.

DIPLOMAT ($$–$$$)
Large, immaculate, modern hotel, not quite in Hradčany but only 10 minutes (uphill) on foot from the castle. A business traveler's favorite, with conference facilities, conveniently located on the route from the airport and next door to a Metro station a mere three stops from downtown.
✚ C3 ✉ Evropská 15, Dejvice ☎ 24 39 41 11 🚇 Dejvická

HOFFMEISTER ($$$)
In a refurbished historic building, this luxurious hotel prides itself on its personalized service. It's enviably sited on the road up to Prague Castle.
✚ D3 ✉ Pod bruskou 7 ☎ 56 18 15 5–7 🚇 Malostranská

KAMPA ($$)
In a delightful corner of the Lesser Town close to the Devil's Brook, this old building is popular with tour groups.
✚ D4/5 ✉ Všehrdova 16 ☎ 5732 0404 🚋 Tram 12, 22 to Hellichova

PENSION DIENTZENHOFER ($$)
In a secluded side street, the former home of the Dientzenhofers, greatest of Prague's Baroque architects.
✚ D4 ✉ Nosticova 2 ☎ 53 16 72 🚋 Tram 12, 22 to Malostranské náměstí

SAVOY ($$$)
Top-of-the-market luxury within easy reach of Prague Castle. Completely modernized.
✚ C4 ✉ Keplerova 6 ☎ 2430 2430 🚋 Tram 22 to Pohořelec

SAX ($$)
You can't get closer to Prague Castle than this little hotel just off Nerudova Street.
✚ C4 ✉ Janský vršek 3 ☎ 53 84 22 or 53 84 98 🚋 Tram 12, 22 to Malostranské náměstí

U PÁVA ($$)
"The Peacock" preens itself on its perfect location by the Vojan Gardens in lower Malá Strana, a few short steps from Charles Bridge.
✚ D4 ✉ U lužického semináře 32 ☎ 5732 0743 🚇 Malostranská

U RAKA PENSION ($$$)
Idyllically located among the stuccoed houses of Nový Svět. Extremely comfortable, rather exclusive.
✚ C3 ✉ Černínská 10 ☎ 2051 1100 🚋 Tram 22 to Brusnice

U TŘÍ PŠTROSŮ ($$$)
"The Three Ostriches," in an exquisite gabled Renaissance building, was once the center of a flourishing feather trade, later a coffeehouse. From some rooms you can almost exchange a

Book ahead
Until recently, Prague suffered from an acute shortage of hotel accommodations, particularly in the middle price range, and was not an inexpensive place to stay. The situation has improved, but it is always wise to book well in advance, especially in summer and if you want to stay in the center.

handshake with people passing by on Charles Bridge.

✚ D4 ✉ Dražického náměstí 12 ☎ 5732 0565
🚊 Tram 12, 22 to Malostranské náměstí

OLD TOWN (STARÉ MĚSTO)

The Old Town is linked to the Lesser Town by the superb Gothic Charles Bridge. From the eastern end of the bridge a warren of streets gives a good idea of what medieval Prague was like, and the Royal Way leads through the center to the Old Town Square.

BETLEM CLUB ($–$$)
Small hotel offering accommodations in the same square as Jan Hus's historic Bethlehem Chapel.

✚ E4 ✉ Betlémské náměstí 9
☎ 24 21 68 72 🚇 Národní třída

CENTRAL ($–$$)
Somewhat run-down but quite adequate. Behind the Municipal House.

✚ E4 ✉ Rybná 8 ☎ 24 81 20 41 or 24 81 27 34
🚇 Náměstí Republiky

CLOISTER INN ($)
Basic accommodations in what was part of State Security's malevolent empire.

✚ E4/5 ✉ Bartolomějská 9
☎ 232 12 89 🚇 Národní třída

INTERCONTINENTAL ($$$)
The epitome of pretension in Communist days and hypermodern

when it opened back in the 1970s. Every comfort as well as spacious public rooms furnished with antiques.

✚ E4 ✉ Náměstí Curieových 5
☎ 24 88 11 11
🚇 Staroměstská

PAŘÍŽ ($$$)
Rampant early-1900s splendor.

✚ E4 ✉ U Obecního domu 1
☎ 24 22 21 51 🚇 Náměstí Republiky

U KRÁLE JIŘÍHO ($)
A small hotel just off the Royal Way with comfortable rooms and the dubious bonus of a pub on the ground floor.

✚ E4 🚇 Liliová 10 ☎ 24 22 20 13 🚇 Staroměstská

UNGELT ($$$)
Apartment hotel in ancient premises that once formed part of the city's customs house.

✚ E4 ✉ Štupartská 1 ☎ 24 81 13 30 🚇 Náměstí Republiky

NEW TOWN (NOVÉ MĚSTO) AND NEARBY

"New" in the 14th century, but developed in the late 19th and early 20th centuries, this part of Prague centers on Wenceslas Square and the broad streets of Narodní and Na příkopě

ADRIA ($$$)
A stunningly restored old establishment amid the glitter of Wenceslas Square.

✚ E5 ✉ Václavské náměstí 26
☎ 24 21 65 43 or 24 23 13 80
🚇 Můstek

Special offers
The number of moderately priced hotels has increased rapidly, but these properties are probably still outnumbered by expensive hotels. However, it's always worth checking to see if the latter are offering any special deals, particularly for weekend stays.

Breathe freely

Choosing a place to stay requires care. A central location may turn out to be noisy with traffic as the rush hour gets under way shortly after 5AM. Somewhere in the suburbs may seem a long way from the action, but if the hotel is near a Metro station, this is unlikely to be a problem, and your night's rest may be more relaxed because you are breathing air that is fresher (albeit marginally so).

AMETYST ($$–$$$)

A fresh and inviting medium-sized, family-owned hotel, the equal in luxury to most of the big names and only 10 minutes' walk from Wenceslas Square.

✚ F6 ✉ Jana Masaryka 11, Vinohrady ☎ 2425 4185 Ⓜ Náměstí Míru

ANNA ($–$$)

A reliable small hotel in the pleasant inner suburb of Vinohrady, less than a quarter of an hour's stroll from Wenceslas Square.

✚ G5 ✉ Budečská 17, Vinohrady ☎ 25 41 63 Ⓜ Náměstí Míru

ATLANTIK ($$)

A pleasant alternative to the Harmony if you want to stay on this busy shopping street close to downtown.

✚ F4 ✉ Na poříčí 9 ☎ 24 81 10 84 Ⓜ Náměstí Republiky

ATRIUM ($$$)

Around the vast interior space that gives this hotel its name are nearly 800 beds, just enough to house President Clinton's entourage when he came to Prague.

✚ F3 ✉ Pobřežní 1 ☎ 24 84 11 11 Ⓜ Florenc

BILÁ LABUŤ ($$)

Run by the reliable Best Western chain.

✚ F4 ✉ Biskupská 9 ☎ 2481 1382 Ⓜ Náměstí Republiky

CITY HOTEL MORAN ($$$)

Austrian-style elegance and comfort in a historic building close to Charles Square.

✚ E6 ✉ Na Moráni 15 ☎ 24 91 52 08 Ⓜ Karlovo náměstí

CITY PENSION ($)

Exceptionally pleasant and one Metro stop from Wenceslas Square.

✚ F6 ✉ Belgická 10 ☎ 691 13 34 Ⓜ Náměstí Míru

EVROPA ($–$$)

Nothing could be closer to Prague's heart than this art-nouveau jewel on Wenceslas Square. But most rooms fail to live up to the promise of the façade.

✚ E5 ✉ Václavské náměstí 25 ☎ 24 22 81 17 Ⓜ Můstek

HARMONY ($$)

A 1930s building just east of the Municipal House providing pleasant accommodations.

✚ F4 ✉ Na poříčí 31 ☎ 23 20 016 Ⓜ Náměstí Republiky

HOTEL 16 U SV. KATEŘINY ($–$$)

Excellent-value family hotel just around the corner from the Dvořák Museum and a 10-minute walk from Wenceslas Square.

✚ E5 ✉ Kateřinská 16 ☎ 29 53 29 or 29 13 13 Ⓜ I. P. Pavlova

JALTA ($$$)

The airconditioned Jalta is a fine example of 1950s architecture, and has an unbeatable position towards the top of Wenceslas Square.

✚ F5 ✉ Václavské náměstí 45 ☎ 2422 9133 Ⓜ Muzeum or Můstek

PALACE ($$$)

A sumptous art-nouveau exterior conceals the completely refurbished ultramodern interior of Prague's priciest hotel.

➕ E4 ✉ Panská 12
☎ 24 09 31 11 🚇 Můstek

PÁV ($$)

A family-run pension in a side street where you'll also find Prague's most popular beer hall.

➕ E5 ✉ Křemencova 13
☎ 24 91 32 86 🚇 Národní třída

THE SUBURBS

Beyond the four historic districts is a ring of suburbs, some dull, but most with their own attractions.

BILÝ LEV ($$)

A good-value establishment in the eastern suburb of Žižkov.

➕ G4 ✉ Cimburkova 20
☎ 27 11 26 🚋 Trams 5, 9, 26 to Husinecká

COUBERTIN ($)

Small modern hotel named after the founder of the modern Olympics, and located among the Strahov sports facilities.

➕ B5 ✉ Atletická 4, Strahov
☎ 35 28 51 🚇 Dejvická, then Bus 149, 217

FORUM ($$$)

International luxury and all that that implies in a steel and glass tower overlooking the Nusle expressway bridge in Vyšehrad. Wenceslas Square is just five minutes away by Metro.

➕ F7 ✉ Kongresová 1, Vyšehrad ☎ 61 19 11 11
🚇 Vyšehrad

GOLF ($)

Large motel handily located on the main road that heads into the city from the west.

➕ Off map to west of Prague
✉ Plzeňská 215 ☎ 52 32 51

HOLIDAY INN PRAGUE ($$)

Unique and long-established. In a Socialist-Realist skyscraper, with all the atmosphere of the Stalinist 1950s.

➕ C2 ✉ Koulova 15
☎ 24 39 31 11 🚇 Dejvická
🚋 Tram 20, 25 to Podbaba

KAFKA ($)

Good-value accommodations on the wrong side of the tracks in the seedy inner suburb of Žižkov, but only 10 minutes' walk from the main train station and a short tram ride to Wenceslas Square.

➕ G4 ✉ Cimburkova 24
☎ 27 31 01 🚋 Tram 5, 9, 26 to Husinecká

LOUDA ($)

Pleasant pension on a residential road off the main highway to northern Bohemia and eastern Germany.

➕ H1 ✉ Kubišova 10
☎ 688 14 91

OBORA ($$)

Well-appointed small hotel in the royal hunting park and near Hvězda Castle, close to the airport.

➕ Off map to west of Prague ✉ Libocká 271/1
☎ 36 77 79

Botels

An alternative to conventional hotels are the "botels" moored at various points along the banks of the Vltava. However, being rather cramped, they are less romantic than they might sound. One such, close to the Palacký Bridge (Palackého most) on the Smíchov quayside, is the Admirál (► 77).

Home away from home

An economical solution to the problem of accommodations is to stay in a private house or, more likely, to rent an apartment. Most agencies have such places on their books, and going through one of them is better than allowing yourself to be solicited on arrival. Private rooms can also be booked from abroad. Check that you won't have to change buses and trams three times to get into town from your accommodation.

PRAHA ($$$)

The Praha perfectly expresses how Communist taste moved from the Stalinist certainties of the International Hotel in the 1950s (now the Holiday Inn; ➤ 85) to the anonymous luxury of the 1970s. Until 1989, the Praha, in its hilltop location in the western suburb of Dejvice, was reserved for privileged and powerful Party people and their guests.
🔢 B2 ✉ Sušická 20, Dejvice
☎ 2434 1111 Ⓜ Dejvická
🚊 Tram 2, 20, 26 to Hadovka

VILA VOYTA ($$$)

This splendid Secession villa in the southern suburbs caters to its mostly business clientele with great care and attention.
➕ Off map to south of Prague
✉ K novému dvoru 124/54, Lhotka ☎ 472 27 60

ACCOMMODATIONS ADVICE

Any number of agencies stand ready to help you with advice on accommodations.
AVE is one of the best established, with offices at the airport, the main train station (✉ Hlavní nádraží, Wilsonova 8 ☎ 24 22 35 21), and Holešovice train station.

Prague Information Service (Pražská informační služba – PIS ☎ 2448 2202), the official city information agency, will also find lodgings. It has offices at the main train station, Old Town Square and Na příkopě (➤ 19).

PRAGUE
travel facts

Arriving & Departing

Before you go
- Visas are not required for citizens of the United States.

When to go
- The best times to visit are in spring, when the fruit trees of Petřín Hill are in blossom, and in early summer.
- Winter weather can be depressingly gray and cold, with high levels of air pollution.
- High summer can become oppressively hot and humid, with considerable rainfall.

Arriving by air
- There are direct flights to Ruzyně Airport from New York and Montréal.
- Prague is served by ČSA, the national airline, as well as by other major carriers.
- The best downtown link is by airport bus, either to Dejvická Metro station or to Náměstí Republiky on the eastern edge of the Old Town. An ordinary city bus is marginally less expensive but meanders all over the suburbs. For taxis, ➤ 91.
- The ČSA main office is at ✉ V celnici 5, Staré město ☎ 2010 4111.

Arriving by train
- Express trains link Prague to all neighboring countries, as well as to Paris and to Ostend in Belgium (ferry connection with Dover in England).
- Most trains terminate at the main station (Hlavní nádraží ✚ F4), though some stop (or terminate) at Holešovice in the northern suburbs or at Smíchov in the southern suburbs, both of which have good onward connections by Metro.

- Czech Railways (ČD) has an information office at the north end of level 3 in the main railway station ☎ 2422 4200.

Arriving by car
- Good main roads link Prague to all neighboring countries, and the motorway linking it with Plžen (Pilsen) and the border with Bavaria is almost complete. Prague is less than 700 miles from Calais, with its frequent ferry services to Dover as well as the Channel Tunnel Shuttle.

Arriving by bus
- Express buses link Prague with international destinations, including London.
- The coach terminal is at Florenc, on the eastern edge of downtown, where there is a Metro station.
- Departure tickets can be obtained at Florenc, but it is easier to buy them through a travel agency.

Arriving by boat
- Occasional passenger boats ply the Vltava and Elbe to Dresden and on to Hamburg.

Customs regulations
- The duty-free allowance comprises 200 cigarettes or 100 cigars or 250g tobacco; 2 liters of wine; 1 liter of liquor; 50ml perfume, and 250ml eau de toilette.
- There is no limit on the import or export of foreign currencies.
- In principle, there are strict limits on the export of goods purchased in the Czech Republic, but the normal tourist souvenirs are unlikely to pose any problem. However, antiques and "rare cultural objects" require an official certificate from a recognized museum or art gallery (which the dealer may already have obtained).

ESSENTIAL FACTS

Travel insurance

- Check your insurance policies to make sure you will be covered for accident, illness, loss, and other eventualities.

Opening hours

- Banks: Mon–Fri 9–5. Komerční banka ⊠ Na příkopě 3 is open Mon–Fri 8–5, and Česká spořitelna ⊠ Václavské náměstí 16 is open Mon–Fri 8–6.
- Stores: Mon–Fri 9–6; Sat 9–1. Food stores may open as early as 7AM; there is some late shopping (to 8PM) on Thu. Some shops in tourist areas also open on Sun.
- Museums and galleries: Tue–Sun 9/10–5. They close Mon, except the National Museum (open Mon and closed Tue) and the Strahov Library (open every day). Some also close for lunch.

National holidays

- January 1, Easter Monday, May 1 (Labor Day), May 8 (Liberation Day), July 5 (SS Cyril and Methodius), July 6 (Jan Hus's Day), October 28 (Independence Day), December 24–26.

Money matters

- The Czech crown (*koruna česká* or Kč) is divided into 100 virtually worthless hellers (*halér*).
- There are coins for 10, 20, and 50 hellers, and for 1, 2, 5, 10, 20, and 50 crowns, and notes in denominations of 20, 50, 100, 200, 500, 1,000, 2,000, and 5,000 crowns.
- There are plenty of bureaux de change, but banks usually give better rates of exchange.
- Credit cards are in increasing use, particularly in places frequented by tourists.

Etiquette

- Czech manners tend to be formal. Titles such as Doctor and Professor must not be ignored, and hands should be shaken when offered.
- Dress is less formal than it used to be; neat casual wear is usually acceptable, though the opera requires a modicum of formality.
- Diners share tables in crowded restaurants, and exchange greetings such as "*dobrý den*" ("good day"), "*dobrou chuť*" ("enjoy your meal"), "*na zdraví!*" ("cheers!") and "*na shledanou*" ("goodbye") at the appropriate moments.
- If you are invited into a Czech home, take flowers or a small gift, and offer to take your shoes off before entering.

Women travelers

- Women travelers need take no more than the usual precautions when visiting Prague.
- Unaccompanied females lingering at night in parts of Wenceslas Square may be taken for prostitutes.

Places of worship

- Roman Catholic: St. Joseph's Church (sv. Josefa) ⊠ Josefská 4, Malá Strana 🔘 Malostranská 🔘 English mass Sun 10:30AM.
- Anglican: St. Clement's Church (sv. Klimenta) ⊠ Klimentská, north Nové město 🔘 Náměstí Republiky 🔘 English-language service Sun 11AM.

Student travelers

- Few discounts are available for students, but keeping out of the most popular tourist spots makes Prague an affordable city to get by in.
- All aspects of youth travel and accommodations are dealt with by

the CKM agency ✉ Jindřišská 28, Nové
město ☎ 26 85 32 Ⓜ Můstek or Náměstí
Republiky.

Time differences

- Central European Time applies
  (seven hours ahead of US
  Standard Time), changed for
  daylight saving between March
  and September.

Toilets

- "WC," "OO," "*muži/páni*" (Men),
  and "*ženy/dámy*" (Women) are
  useful signs to remember.
- Public facilities are rare; look in
  restaurants, cafés, etc.
- Tip the attendant (usually an old
  woman) with some smaller
  coins—these are her wages.

Electricity

- 230 volts, 50 cycles AC, fed
  through standard Continental
  two-pin plugs.

PUBLIC TRANSPORTATION

- Prague's comprehensive
  transportation system is based on
  the immaculate underground
  Metro and the slightly less pristine
  but equally reliable trams and buses.
- One inexpensive ticket obtained
  at stations, kiosks, and some hotel
  receptions serves all three
  modes and must be validated
  by inserting it into the clipping
  machine as you enter a station
  or board a vehicle. A fresh ticket
  must be used for each change
  of mode.
- The best public transportation
  map is in the city guide available
  from the Prague Information
  Service (► 19). This shows all
  Metro and tram lines and, very
  usefully, names the tram stops as
  well as Metro stations.

- Expect crowding during the rush
  hours (although they start and
  finish earlier than in many
  Western countries). The young
  and fit should give up their seats
  to the elderly, pregnant women,
  and people with disabilities.

Metro

- This showpiece system, with its
  fast and frequent trains and
  clean stations, consists of three
  lines: A (color-coded green), B
  (yellow), and C (red). They
  converge from the suburbs
  onto downtown where there are
  several interchange stations.
- To ensure you get on the right
  train, check the line (A, B, or
  C) and note the name of the
  terminus station at the end of
  the line in the direction you
  wish to travel; this station
  appears on the overhead
  direction signs.
- Outlying stations are relatively far
  apart and are intended more to
  feed commuters to connecting
  trams and buses than to take
  tourists to their favorite spots.
- Particularly useful stations are
  Můstek (for Wenceslas Square
  and Old Town Square),
  Staroměstská (for Old Town
  Square), and Malostranská (for
  Malá Strana and for Tram No. 22).
  Hradčanská station is quite a
  long walk from Prague Castle.

Tram

- The tramway system operates
  in close conjunction with its
  underground equivalent. It is
  worthwhile studying the route
  map, because travel by tram can
  spare your legs on many of your
  likely itineraries.
- The name of every tram stop
  appears on the stop sign and on
  the route map.

- Tram routes are numbered, and the tram has a destination board. Timetables are usually pasted on the stop and are almost always adhered to.
- There is a skeleton service of night trams, with a system of numbers and schedules that differs from that operating during the daytime.
- A particularly useful and scenic line is the No. 22, which runs from downtown (at Národní třída) right through Malá Strana, past Malostranská Metro station, then climbs to the back entrance of Prague Castle (Pražský hrad stop) or continues on to Strahov Monastery.

Bus

- Kept out of the downtown to minimize pollution, buses serve all the suburban areas that the trams do not reach.

Discounts

- Special passes are valid for periods of one day upwards. They are useful only if you intend to make lots of trips—more than about eight a day.

Taxi

- Prague taxi drivers have an appalling reputation for overcharging and being disagreeable.
- Agree on the fare beforehand. Ask for a receipt to reduce excessive demands.
- It may be better to flag down a moving taxi rather than go to a taxi stand.
- For taxis, telephone AAA Radiotaxi ☎ 1080 or Profitaxi ☎ 1035.
- The more upscale hotels have their own taxi service, reliable but expensive.

MEDIA & COMMUNICATIONS

Telephones

- The Czech Republic's phone system is being modernized, and making calls can be very frustrating. All Prague subscribers have been, or are being, allotted new numbers.
- Most public phones now take phone cards, on sale in kiosks and post offices in denominations of Kč150 upwards.
- Beware that telephoning from your hotel may cost up to four times the standard rate.

Mail

- Postage stamps can be bought not only at post offices but also at kiosks and hotel receptions.
- The main post office, with fax and poste restante services, is at ✚ F4 ✉ Jindřišská 14, Nové město ☎ 24 22 88 56 Ⓜ Můstek.

Newspapers and magazines

- Foreign-language newspapers are on sale at downtown newsstands and at some hotel reception desks.
- The leading English-language publication is the weekly *Prague Post*, with useful events listings.
- The English-language *Central European Business Weekly* is much as its title suggests.
- The German-language weekly *Prager Zeitung* is for the Czech republic's minuscule German population.

Radio and television

- Local TV consists of four channels—ČT1 and ČT2 (state-owned), and Nova and Prima (private). None is likely to be of interest to those who don't speak Czech. Major hotels have multiple satellite channels.

- Local Radio 1 (91.9 FM) airs news of tourist interest in English at 3:30PM on weekdays.
- Voice of America and the BBC World Service can be picked up on 106.2 FM and 1197kHz MW respectively.
- Most local stations play rock's "golden oldies". Country Radio (89.5 FM) plays country music; Radio 1 (91.9 FM) plays avant-garde rock; and Classic FM (98.7 FM) plays classical music.

EMERGENCIES

Sensible precautions

- Despite some horror stories, Prague is still safer than most comparable Western cities.
- The main hazard is pickpockets in the tourist areas—Wenceslas Square, Charles Bridge, and Old Town Square. Hold onto your handbag and don't carry your wallet or passport in your back pocket.
- A common scam is for someone to accost you with an innocent-seeming enquiry about money or the location of the nearest bank. His "policeman" accomplice will then appear and relieve you of your passport if you are unwise enough to produce it.

Lost property

- The lost property office is at ✉ Karoliny Světlé 5, Staré město ☎ 24 23 50 85.

Medical treatment

- Emergency medical treatment is done under contract, so check your insurance policies in advance of your trip.

- Foreigners' Polyclinic
  ✉ Roentgenova 2, Motol (off map) ☎ 52 92 21 46 ☐ Tram 4, 7, 9, 58, or Bus 167 from Anděl Metro. Bring your passport to this former Communist Party clinic, which is part of the Nemocnice, Na Homolce, the huge hospital complex just off the main highway to Pilsen in the western suburb of Motol. It is the best place to go for serious treatment.
- Fakultní poliklinika ✚ E5 ✉ Karlovo náměstí 32, Nové město ☎ 2490 4111 ☐ Karlovo náměstí. A downtown alternative to the above for less serious ailments.
- Drugs prescribed locally must be paid for.
- Remember to bring supplies of any regular medication you take with you.
- 24-hour pharmacies are at ✉ Palackého 5 and ✉ Belgická 37.

Emergency phone numbers

- Ambulance ☎ 155.
- Police ☎ 158.
- Fire brigade ☎ 150.

Embassy

- USA: ✚ D4 ✉ Tržiště 15, Malá Strana ☎ 5732 0355 ☐ Malostranská, then Tram 12, 22.

LANGUAGE

- Czech is a Slavic language, so anyone who knows other Slavic languages, such as Russian or Polish, should have little difficulty in muddling through.
- It will be rewarding to master a few words and phrases, if only to be able to ask if anyone speaks your language and to recognize some signs.
- Czech is pronounced as it is written (unlike English).

Vowels

a	as in mammoth	á	as in father
é	as in air	e	as in yes
i,y	as in city	í,ý	as in meet
o	as in top	ó	as in more
u	as in book	ů	as in boom

Consonants

c as in its č as in china
ch as in Scottish loch
j as in yes n as in onion
r rolled or trilled r ř combination
of r and z (as
š as in shine in Dvořák)
z as in zero ž as in pleasure

Basic words and phrases

yes ano
no ne
please prosím
thank you děkuji
do you speak English/German?
  mluvíte anglicky /německy?
I don't understand nerozumím
I don't speak Czech nemluvím česky
hello ahoj
good morning/good day dobrý den
goodbye na shledanou
sorry promiňte
where? kde?
how much? kolik?
when? kdy?
what? co?

Days of the week

Monday pondělí Friday pátek
Tuesday uterý Saturday sobota
Wednesday středa Sunday neděle
Thursday čvrtek

Months of the year

January leden July červenec
February únor August srpen
March březen September září
April duben October říjen
May květen November listopad
June červen December prosinec

Useful words

beer pivo
big velký/á/é
bus or tram stop zastávka
café kavárna
castle hradhrad
closed zavřeno
Danger! pozor!
entrance vchod/vstup
exit východ/výstup
forbidden zákaz
market trh
open otevřeno
pharmacy lékarna
pull (sign on door) sem
push (sign on door) tam
small malý/á/é
station nádraží
water voda

Numbers

1	jeden/jedna/	15	patnáct
	jedno	16	šestnáct
2	dva/dvě	17	sedmnáct
3	tři	18	osmnáct
4	čtyři	19	devatenáct
5	pět	20	dvacet
6	šest	30	třicet
7	sedm	40	čtyřicet
8	osm	50	padesát
9	devět	60	šedesát
10	deset	70	sedmdesát
11	jedenáct	80	osmdesát
12	dvanáct	90	devadesát
13	třináct	100	sto
14	čtrnáct	1,000	tisíc

INDEX

Citypack
Prague

While every care has been taken to ensure the accuracy of the information in this guide, time brings change, and consequently the publisher cannot accept responsibility for errors that may occur. Prudent travelers will therefore want to call ahead to verify prices and other "perishable" information.

Published in the United States by Fodor's Travel Publications
Published in the United Kingdom by AA Publishing

Fodor's is a registered trademark of Random House Inc.

ISBN 0–679–00252–9
Second Edition

FODOR'S CITYPACK PRAGUE

AUTHOR *Michael Ivory*
ORIGINAL DESIGN *Design FX*
COPY EDITOR *Audrey Horne*
VERIFIER *Nick Parsons*
INDEXER *Marie Lorimer*

CARTOGRAPHY *The Automobile Association*
RV Reise- und Verkehrsverlag
COVER DESIGN *Fabrizio La Rocca,*
Allison Salztman
SECOND EDITION UPDATED BY
OutHouse Publishing Services

Acknowledgments

The Automobile Association wishes to thank the following photographers, associations, and libraries for their assistance in the preparation of this book: M. IVORY 25a, 25b; NATIONAL GALLERY IN PRAGUE 27, 41b, 47; REX FEATURES LTD 12. All remaining pictures are held in the Association's own library (AA PHOTO LIBRARY), with contributions from C. Sawyer 1, 2, 5b, 13a, 13b, 18, 19, 20, 26b, 28a, 29, 30a, 32b, 36b, 37, 38b, 41a, 48a, 49b, 50, 52, 54, 55, 56, 58, 61b, 87b; A. SOUTER 5a, 7, 23b, 24, 33, 34, 36a, 42a, 46a, 46b, 87a; J. WYAND 6, 16, 17, 21a, 21b, 23a, 26a, 27, 28b, 30b, 31, 32a, 35a, 35b, 38a, 39, 40, 42b, 43, 44a, 44b, 45, 48b, 49a, 51, 57, 61a.

Color separation by Daylight Colour Art Pte Ltd, Singapore
Manufactured by Dai Nippon Printing Co. (Hong Kong) Ltd
10 9 8 7 6 5 4 3 2

Titles in the Citypack series
● Amsterdam ● Atlanta ● Beijing ● Berlin ● Boston ● Chicago ● Dublin●
● Florence ● Hong Kong ● London ● Los Angeles ● Miami ● Montréal ●
● New York ● Paris ● Prague ● Rome ● San Francisco ● Seattle ●Shanghai ●
● Sydney ● Tokyo ● Toronto ● Venice ● Vienna ● Washington D.C. ●